French

THE AUSTRALIAN
Women's Weekly

French

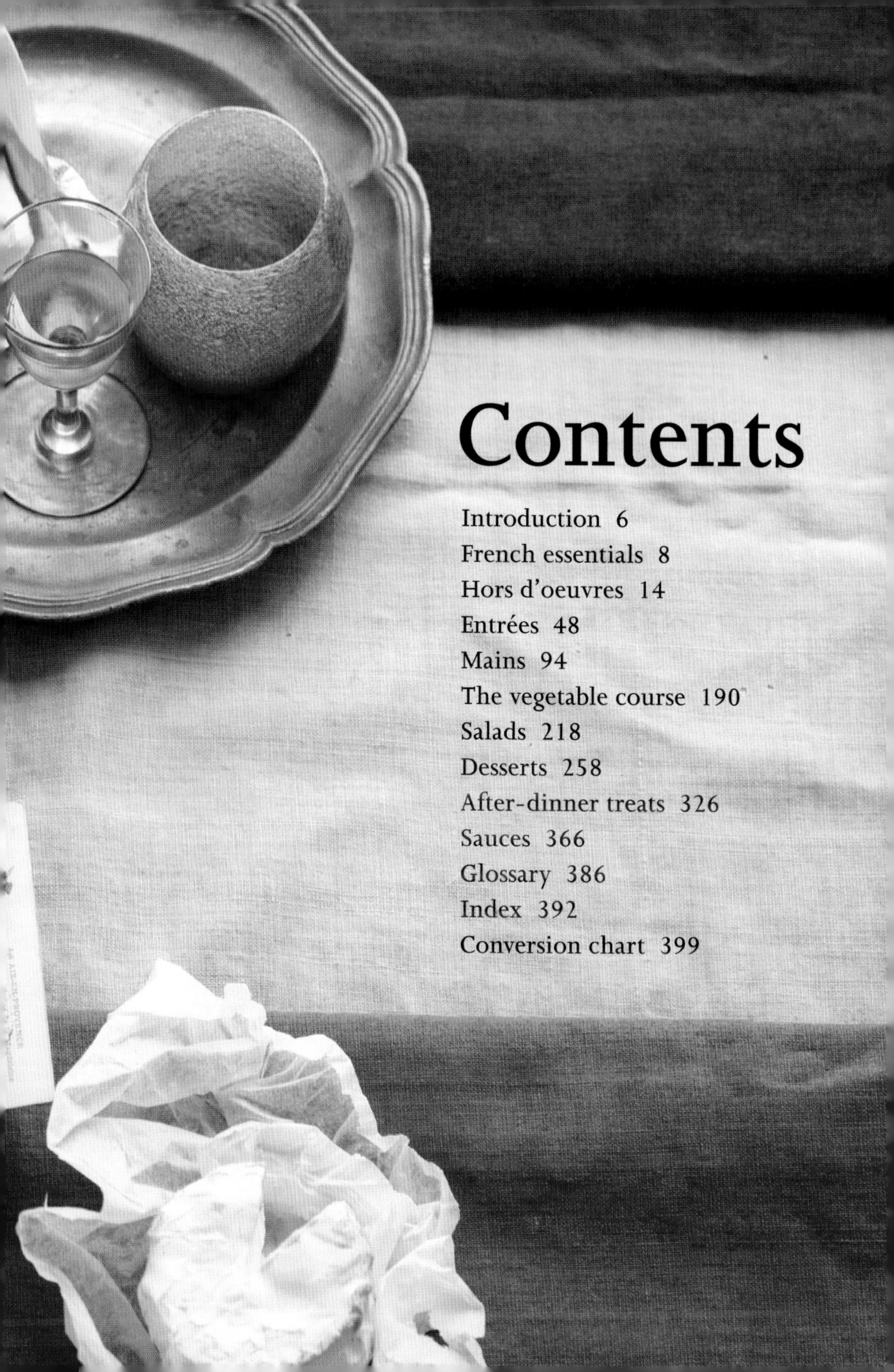

Contents

French food is loved – and cooked – around the world. It's because the French take such pride in their food and give its preparation such time and care that the dishes they create are so delicious and so universally loved.

In France every meal is savoured as a fundamental part of life. Recipes are passed down through generations, and family traditions are a treasured part of their culture. Fresh, seasonal produce is at the heart of French cooking – this is seen most obviously in the peasant food of the provinces where only local ingredients are used and many of these dishes are now cooked in kitchens far away from

France. Salade niçoise, bouillabaisse, boeuf bourguignon, quiche lorraine – you'll see these on café and restaurant menus from New York to Nairobi. The French like to eat several courses – hors d'oeuvres, entrée, main course, vegetables or salad as a separate course, cheese and then dessert. It sounds like a lot of food but they eat small quantities and make the meal last for a couple of hours. It's a relaxed, civilised way to approach mealtimes.

French food culture is about slowing down and savouring the pleasure of good food. Let us take you on a gastronomic journey through the best that French cuisine has to offer. Bon appétit!

French essentials

CREME FRAICHE

Crème fraîche translates from french as "fresh cream". It is a fermented cream with a slightly tangy, nutty flavour and velvety texture and can be used in both sweet and savoury dishes, in much the same way as sour cream. It has the advantage of boiling without curdling. It contains at least 35% butterfat.

DIJON MUSTARD

Also called french mustard. Pale brown, creamy, distinctively flavoured, fairly mild french mustard. It is an essential ingredient in French dressings, sauces and marinades.

CORNICHONS

French for gherkin, a very small variety of cucumber. Pickled, they are a traditional accompaniment to pâté, and are also served with a plate of charcuterie (cold meats), fondue or raclette. They are essential to a French picnic.

LENTILS DU PUY OR PUY GREEN LENTILS

Green-blue (nearly black), tiny lentils with a nutty, earthy flavour and a hardy nature that allows them to be rapidly cooked without disintegrating. French-style green lentils grown in Victoria, are a local cousin to the expensive French import.

BRIE CHEESE

Is a soft cow's milk cheese named after Brie, the French province in which it originated (north-east of Paris). It is very soft, pale in colour with a rind of white mould (which is typically eaten). It is sold cut into wedges from a large wheel. Brie has a rich, sweet flavour that varies from buttery to mushroomy, and a heavy, creamy texture (at its best served at room temperature).

CAMEMBERT CHEESE

Is a soft cow's milk cheese made in Normandy (northern France). It is soft, pale yellow in colour with a rind of white mould with pale orangey streaks (which is typically eaten). It is sold in small wooden boxes. It's at its best served at room temperature and matured to the heart of the cheese (creamy right through).

BAGUETTE

A French icon, it has a crisp golden crust and white, soft filling. It is recognisable by its elongated shape and weighs about 250g. It is the type of bread most eaten in France: either halved with butter for breakfast, with a main meal at lunch or dinner, as a sandwich or after school with some chocolate.

SHALLOTS

Also called french shallots, eschalots or golden shallots, these are small, elongated, brown-skinned members of the onion family that grow in tight clusters similar to garlic. They are used in sauces, added to salads for extra punch, roasted or caramelised and served with steak.

Mirepoix

20g (¾ ounce) butter
1 small carrot (70g), diced
1 small onion (80g), diced
1 stalk celery (150g), trimmed, diced
50g (1½ ounces) speck, diced
1 sprig fresh thyme
⅓ cup (80ml) dry white wine

1 Melt butter in large saucepan; cook carrot, onion, celery, speck and thyme until vegetables soften. Season to taste. Stir in wine; cook until nearly evaporated.

prep + cook time 15 minutes **makes** 1 cup
nutritional count per ¼ cup 5.9g total fat (3.4g saturated fat); 380kJ (91 cal); 2.4g carbohydrate; 3.4g protein; 1.2g fibre
tips Invented in the 18th century by the Duc of Levis-Mirepoix, mirepoix has since become a classic preparation of French cooking. It is the aromatic base for stews, soups and sauces. There are many recipes (with or without speck, adding a little leek) but the main thing is that all the vegetables (and speck if using) are coarsely diced (around 1cm/½-inch cubes) and that the ratio of mirepoix to meat, if using in a stew, is around 1 to 10.

Fines herbes

1 tablespoon finely chopped fresh tarragon
1 tablespoon finely chopped fresh chervil
1 tablespoon finely chopped fresh parsley
1 tablespoon finely chopped fresh chives

1 Combine herbs in small bowl.

prep time 5 minutes **makes** ⅓ cup
nutritional count per tablespoon 0g total fat (0g saturated fat); 4kJ (1 cal); 0g carbohydrate; 0g protein; 0.2g fibre
tips Add at end of cooking if adding to stews or sauces. Great for simple green leaf salads, omelettes, soufflés or butter.

Chicken stock

2kg (4 pounds) chicken bones
2 medium brown onions (300g), chopped coarsely
2 stalks celery (300g), trimmed, chopped coarsely
2 medium carrots (240g), chopped coarsely
3 bay leaves
2 teaspoons black peppercorns
5 litres (20 cups) water

1 Place ingredients in large saucepan or boiler; simmer, uncovered, 2 hours, skimming surface occasionally. Strain stock through muslin-lined sieve or colander into large heatproof bowl; discard solids. Cool. Cover; refrigerate until cold. Skim and discard surface fat before using.

prep + cook time 2 hours 10 minutes (+ cooling & refrigeration)
makes 3.5 litres (14 cups)
nutritional count per 1 cup (250ml) 0.6g total fat (0.2g saturated fat); 105kJ (25 cal); 2.3g carbohydrate; 1.9g protein; 1.1g fibre
tip Freeze the stock in 1- or 2-cup portions in resealable plastic bags.

Shortcrust pastry

1¾ cups (260g) plain (all-purpose) flour
155g (5 ounces) cold butter, chopped coarsely
1 egg yolk
2 teaspoons lemon juice
⅓ cup (80ml) iced water, approximately

1 Sift flour into bowl; rub in butter. Add egg yolk, juice and enough water to make ingredients cling together.
2 Knead gently on floured surface until smooth. Cover; refrigerate 30 minutes.

prep time 15 minutes (+ refrigeration) **makes** 450g (14½ ounces)
nutritional count per 450g (14½ ounces) 135.9g total fat (86g saturated fat); 8845kJ (2116 cal); 188.6g carbohydrate; 32.2g protein; 9.9g fibre
tip If using a food processor, process flour and butter until crumbly. With motor running, add egg yolk, juice and enough water to make ingredients come together as a ball.

Hors d’oeuvres

Chicken liver pâté

1kg (2 pounds) chicken livers
200g (6½ ounces) ghee (clarified butter)
4 rindless bacon slices (260g)
1 small brown onion (80g), chopped finely
¼ cup (60ml) brandy
½ cup (125ml) pouring cream
2 teaspoons finely chopped fresh thyme
pinch ground nutmeg

1 Cut any sinew from livers; pull each lobe away from connecting tissue.
2 Heat a quarter of the ghee in large frying pan; cook half the livers, stirring, until browned and barely cooked. Remove from pan. Repeat with another quarter of the ghee and remaining livers.
3 Heat 1 tablespoon of the remaining ghee in same pan; cook bacon and onion, stirring, until onion softens. Add brandy; bring to the boil.
4 Blend livers, bacon mixture, cream, thyme, nutmeg and 2 tablespoons of the remaining ghee until smooth (you may need to do this in batches).
5 Press pâté into 1-litre (4-cup) dish; melt remaining ghee, pour over pâté in dish. Refrigerate 3 hours or overnight.

prep + cook time 45 minutes (+ refrigeration) **makes** 4 cups
nutritional count per teaspoon 1.7g total fat (1g saturated fat); 88kJ (21 cal); 0.1g carbohydrate; 1.2g protein; 0g fibre
serving suggestion Lavosh crispbread, melba toast or water crackers.

Terrine de campagne

350g (11¾ ounces) chicken thigh fillets, chopped coarsely
400g (13 ounces) boned pork belly, rind removed, chopped coarsely
280g (9 ounces) calves' liver, trimmed, chopped coarsely
3 rindless bacon slices (195g), chopped coarsely
3 cloves garlic, crushed
2 teaspoons finely chopped fresh thyme
10 juniper berries, crushed
2 tablespoons port
¼ cup (60ml) dry white wine
1 egg, beaten lightly

1 Preheat oven to 150°C/300°F. Oil 1.5-litre (6-cup) ovenproof terrine dish.
2 Chop or process meats, separately, until coarsely minced; combine in large bowl with remaining ingredients.
3 Press meat mixture into terrine dish; cover with foil. Place terrine dish in baking dish; pour enough boiling water into baking dish to come halfway up side of terrine dish. Cook 1 hour. Uncover; cook further 1 hour.
4 Remove terrine dish from baking dish; cover terrine with baking paper. Weight with another dish filled with heavy cans; cool 10 minutes then refrigerate overnight.
5 Turn terrine onto serving plate; allow reach to room temperature. Serve terrine sliced.

prep + cook time 2 hours 20 minutes (+ refrigeration) **serves** 6
nutritional count per serving 28.6g total fat (9.6g saturated fat); 1839kJ (440 cal); 2.5g carbohydrate; 40.4g protein; 0.3g fibre
serving suggestion Cornichons and slices of french bread.

Chicken liver and asparagus terrine

12 slices prosciutto (180g)
¼ cup (60ml) olive oil
1 large brown onion (200g), chopped finely
4 cloves garlic, crushed
¼ cup (60ml) pouring cream
250g (8 ounces) mushrooms, sliced thinly
⅓ cup (25g) coarsely grated parmesan cheese
400g (12½ ounces) chicken livers, halved, trimmed
700g (1½ pounds) minced (ground) chicken
250g (8 ounces) asparagus, trimmed

1 Preheat oven to 180°C/530°F. Oil 1.5-litre (6-cup) ovenproof terrine dish.
2 Line base and sides of dish with prosciutto slices, allowing 7cm (2½-inch) overhang on long sides of dish.
3 Heat 1 tablespoon of the oil in large frying pan; cook onion and garlic, stirring, until onion softens. Stir in cream; transfer to medium bowl.
4 Heat 1 tablespoon of the remaining oil in same pan; cook mushrooms, stirring, until browned. Stir in cheese; transfer to another medium bowl.
5 Heat remaining oil in same pan; cook liver, stirring, over high heat, about 2 minutes or until browned, but not cooked through. Drain on absorbent paper.
6 Add liver and chicken to onion mixture in medium bowl; stir to combine. Spread one-third of the chicken mixture in terrine dish; arrange asparagus on top. Cover with another third of the chicken mixture; top with mushroom mixture, then top with remaining chicken mixture. Fold prosciutto slices over to cover chicken mixture.
7 Bake terrine about 1 hour or until chicken is cooked through. Remove from oven; drain juices from dish. Stand 20 minutes in dish before slicing.

prep + cook time 1 hour 45 minutes (+ cooling) **serves** 8
nutritional count per serving 21.6g total fat (7g saturated fat); 1438kJ (344 cal); 3.3g carbohydrate; 33.6g protein; 1.8g fibre

Pork rillettes with witlof and cornichons

1kg (2 pounds) boned pork belly, rind removed, cut into chunks
3 bay leaves
2 cloves garlic, chopped coarsely
¼ cup (60ml) dry white wine
¼ cup (60ml) water
2 teaspoons salt
1 teaspoon ground black pepper
1 small red onion (100g), chopped finely
1 tablespoon finely chopped fresh flat-leaf parsley
6 witlof (belgian endive) (750g), trimmed, leaves separated
⅔ cup (120g) drained cornichons

1 Preheat oven to 150°C/300°F.
2 Combine pork, bay leaves, garlic, wine, the water, salt and pepper in large shallow baking dish.
3 Roast pork mixture, covered, about 2½ hours or until pork is very tender.
4 Discard bay leaves from pork; using two forks, shred pork finely in dish with pan juices. Stir in onion and parsley.
5 Serve pork mixture with witlof and cornichons.

prep + cook time 3 hours **serves** 8
nutritional count per serving 28.1g total fat (9.5g saturated fat); 1551kJ (371 cal); 3.1g carbohydrate; 24.5g protein; 2.8g fibre
tips Rillettes are a classic dish served for an aperitif with slices of baguette, cornichons and a glass of red wine. Duck or goose rillettes are also very popular in France.

Salmon and green peppercorn rillettes

1 long french bread stick (300g)
3 cups (750ml) water
½ cup (125ml) dry white wine
1 small brown onion (80g), chopped coarsely
1 bay leaf
1 teaspoon black peppercorns
315g (10½ ounces) salmon fillets
125g (4 ounces) smoked salmon, sliced thinly
60g (2 ounces) butter, softened
2 teaspoons finely grated lemon rind
1 tablespoon drained green peppercorns in brine, rinsed, chopped coarsely

1 Preheat oven to 160°C/325°F.
2 Cut bread into 1cm (½-inch) slices; toast, uncovered, in single layer, on oven tray in oven about 15 minutes or until bread is dry.
3 Meanwhile, bring the water, wine, onion, bay leaf and black peppercorns to the boil in medium saucepan. Add salmon fillets, reduce heat; simmer, uncovered, about 5 minutes or until almost cooked through. Cool salmon fillets in liquid 5 minutes; drain. Discard cooking liquid.
4 Discard any skin and bones from salmon fillets; place in medium bowl, flake with fork. Add smoked salmon, butter, rind and green peppercorns; stir to combine. Divide salmon mixture among four ½-cup (125ml) dishes; cool to room temperature. Serve with bread slices.

prep + cook time 40 minutes (+ cooling) **serves** 4
nutritional count per serving 22.2g total fat (10g saturated fat); 2144kJ (513 cal); 41.8g carbohydrate; 29.7g protein; 3.1g fibre

Black olive tapenade

2 cups (240g) seeded black olives
1 drained anchovy fillet, rinsed
1 tablespoon drained capers, rinsed
2 teaspoons dijon mustard
2 tablespoons olive oil

1 Rinse olives; drain on absorbent paper. Blend or process olives with anchovy, capers and mustard until smooth.
2 With motor operating, add oil in a thin steady stream, processing until tapenade is smooth.

prep time 5 minutes **makes** 1 cup
nutritional count per tablespoon 3.3g total fat (0.5g saturated fat); 213kJ (51 cal); 4.6g carbohydrate; 0.6g protein; 0.3g fibre
tip This classic Provençal preparation is used as a dip for raw vegetables, a spread on bread and pizza, and served with fish and meats.
serving suggestion Sliced toasted turkish or french bread.

Goat's cheese and zucchini flower quiche

3 sheets shortcrust pastry
12 baby zucchini with flowers (240g)
100g (3 ounces) firm goat's cheese, chopped finely
⅓ cup (25g) finely grated parmesan cheese
2 tablespoons finely chopped garlic chives
1¼ cups (310ml) pouring cream
¼ cup (60ml) milk
3 eggs

1 Preheat oven to 200°C/400°F. Oil 12-hole (⅓-cup/80ml) muffin pan.
2 Using 9cm (3½-inch) cutter, cut 12 rounds from pastry; press rounds into pan holes.
3 Remove flowers from zucchini; remove and discard stamens from flowers, reserve flowers. Slice zucchini thinly. Divide combined sliced zucchini, cheeses and chives into pastry cases.
4 Whisk cream, milk and eggs in large jug; pour into pastry cases. Top each quiche with a zucchini flower.
5 Bake quiches about 25 minutes. Stand in pan 5 minutes before serving.

prep + cook time 50 minutes **makes** 12
nutritional count per quiche 25.8g total fat (15g saturated fat); 1421kJ (340 cal); 19.9g carbohydrate; 7.1g protein; 1.1g fibre
tip It is fine to use just one 300ml carton of cream in this recipe.

Asparagus, tomato and goat's cheese tarts

170g (5½ ounces) asparagus
125g (4 ounces) cherry tomatoes
1 teaspoon finely grated lemon rind
1 tablespoon olive oil
¼ cup lightly packed fresh basil leaves, shredded finely
20 shortcrust or fillo pastry cases
70g (2½ ounces) marinated goat's cheese, drained

1 Trim asparagus; slice thinly. Boil, steam or microwave asparagus until tender; drain. Rinse under cold water; drain.
2 Halve tomatoes; cut into thin wedges.
3 Combine asparagus and tomatoes in medium bowl with rind, oil and half the basil.
4 Spoon half the asparagus mixture into pastry cases; top with cheese, then remaining asparagus mixture. Sprinkle with remaining basil.

prep + cook time 25 minutes **makes** 20
nutritional count per tart 6.1g total fat (2.9g saturated fat); 389kJ (93 cal); 7.7g carbohydrate; 1.8g protein; 0.6g fibre
tip You can prepare asparagus and tomatoes for asparagus mixture up to 8 hours in advance. Cover and refrigerate separately. Assemble tarts just before serving.

Caramelised leek and brie tartlets

1 tablespoon olive oil
25g (¾ ounce) butter
2 medium leeks (700g), sliced finely
1 clove garlic, crushed
1 tablespoon light brown sugar
1 tablespoon white wine vinegar
3 sheets puff pastry
200g (6½-ounce) piece brie cheese
24 sprigs lemon thyme

1 Preheat oven to 200°C/400°F. Oil two 12-hole (2-tablespoons/40ml) deep flat-based patty pans.
2 Heat oil and butter in large frying pan; cook leek, stirring, about 5 minutes or until leek softens. Add garlic, sugar and vinegar; cook, stirring, about 8 minutes or until leek caramelises.
3 Cut eight squares from each pastry sheet; press one pastry square into each pan hole. Spoon leek mixture into pastry cases.
4 Cut cheese into 24 pieces. Place a piece of cheese on each tartlet.
5 Bake tartlets about 20 minutes. Serve tartlets topped with thyme.

prep + cook time 40 minutes **makes** 24
nutritional count per tartlet 8.8g total fat (4.8g saturated fat); 535kJ (128 cal); 8.7g carbohydrate; 3.1g protein; 0.8g fibre
tip We used a 8.5cm (3½-inch) square cutter to make the pastry squares. The cutter is measured from corner to corner.

Camembert with pear compote on pumpernickel

½ cup (75g) dried pears, chopped finely
2 tablespoons dried cranberries, chopped finely
1 cinnamon stick
1 tablespoon caster (superfine) sugar
¼ cup (60ml) water
200g (6½-ounce) whole camembert cheese
24 cocktail pumpernickel rounds (250g)
1 tablespoon roasted pistachios, chopped finely

1 Combine pear, cranberries, cinnamon, sugar and the water in small saucepan; bring to the boil. Reduce heat; simmer, uncovered, 10 minutes. Cool to room temperature. Discard cinnamon.
2 Cut cheese into 24 wedges.
3 Place pumpernickel rounds on serving platter; top each round with a wedge of cheese, ½ teaspoon of the compote then a sprinkle of nuts.

prep + cook time 30 minutes (+ cooling) **makes** 24
nutritional count per piece 2.6g total fat (1.5g saturated fat); 268kJ (64 cal); 8.1g carbohydrate; 2.4g protein; 1.3g fibre
tip You could also use brie for this recipe.

Peppered beef and blue cheese canapés

500g (1-pound) beef fillet, trimmed
¼ cup (60ml) olive oil
2 tablespoons finely cracked black pepper
180g (5½-ounce) packet lavosh crispbreads
3 cups (350g) firmly packed trimmed watercress
blue cheese mousse
100g (3 ounces) blue cheese, softened
100g (3 ounces) cream cheese, softened
⅓ cup (60ml) pouring cream

1 Halve beef lengthways; rub with oil and pepper. Cook beef on heated oiled grill plate (or grill or barbecue) until cooked to your liking, turning beef once. Cover beef; stand 10 minutes before slicing thinly.
2 Meanwhile, make blue cheese mousse.
3 Serve lavosh topped with beef, a spoonful of mousse, and sprigs of watercress.
blue cheese mousse Stir ingredients together until smooth; season to taste.

prep + cook time 30 minutes **makes** 48
nutritional count per piece 4.2g total fat (1.8g saturated fat); 272kJ (65 cal); 2.5g carbohydrate; 4g protein; 0.8g fibre
tip Use a soft creamy blue cheese for the mousse; the mousse can be made a day ahead and kept, covered, in the fridge. It's best to cook the beef as close to serving time as possible.

Mushroom toasties

600g (1 ¼ pounds) mixed mushrooms
2 tablespoons olive oil
40g (1 ½ ounces) butter
3 cloves garlic, crushed
3 sprigs fresh thyme
¼ cup (20g) finely grated parmesan cheese
2 tablespoons finely chopped fresh flat-leaf parsley
2 teaspoons worcestershire sauce
250g (8 ounces) brioche
⅓ cup (80g) sour cream
2 tablespoons finely chopped fresh chives

1 Preheat oven to 150°C/300°F.
2 Process mushrooms until chopped finely.
3 Heat oil and butter in large frying pan; cook garlic, thyme and mushrooms, stirring, until tender. Discard thyme stems. Stir in cheese, parsley and sauce.
4 Cut brioche into 1cm (½-inch) slices, toast both sides in an electric toaster or under a preheated grill (broiler). Cut out 3.5cm (1 ½-inch) rounds from brioche slices, place on oven tray; toast again in oven about 5 minutes or until crisp.
5 Place one teaspoon mushroom mixture on each toast, top with sour cream and chives.

prep + cook time 40 minutes **makes** 48
nutritional count per toastie 2.9g total fat (1.4g saturated fat); 176kJ (42 cal); 2.8g carbohydrate; 1.1g protein; 0.5g fibre
tips Use whatever mushrooms you like: we used a combination of button, swiss brown and oyster mushrooms. Cook mushrooms until juices evaporate, so they don't make the brioche soggy.
You can toast the brioche rounds in oven to dry out up to 7 days ahead. Cool and store in an airtight container. Assemble toasties just before serving.

Asparagus and brie tartines

340g (11 ounces) asparagus spears, trimmed
3 cloves garlic, sliced thinly
1 turkish bread loaf (430g)
200g (6½ ounces) thinly sliced brie cheese

1 Preheat oven to 200°C/400°F.
2 Combine asparagus and garlic in large baking dish; spray with oil-spray. Roast, uncovered, 10 minutes.
3 Meanwhile, cut bread crossways into six pieces; place on oven tray. Heat bread, in oven, 5 minutes.
4 Top bread with asparagus mixture and cheese; bake about 10 minutes or until cheese melts.

prep + cook time 30 minutes **serves** 6
nutritional count per serving 12.5g total fat (6.7g saturated fat); 1287kJ (308 cal); 33g carbohydrate; 14.3g protein; 3g fibre

Cheese and olive loaf (pain aux olives)

1 cup (150g) self-raising flour
⅔ cup (80g) coarsely grated gruyère cheese
2 tablespoons coarsely chopped fresh mint
½ teaspoon ground black pepper
1 cup (120g) seeded green olives, chopped coarsely
75g (2½ ounces) ham, chopped coarsely
4 eggs, beaten lightly
80g (2½ ounces) butter, melted

1 Preheat oven to 200°C/400°F. Oil 8cm x 26cm (3¾-inch x 10½-inch) bar cake pan.
2 Sift flour into medium bowl; add cheese, mint, pepper, olives and ham. Add egg and butter; stir until well combined. Spread mixture into pan.
3 Bake loaf about 35 minutes or until browned lightly. Turn onto wire rack to cool.

prep + cook time 50 minutes **serves** 6
nutritional count per serving 19.4g total fat (11.1g saturated fat); 1329kJ (318 cal); 22.4g carbohydrate; 13.3g protein; 1.3g fibre
tip This loaf is suitable to freeze.

Oysters with tomato and shallot vinaigrette

2 teaspoons red wine vinegar
1 tablespoon olive oil
1 shallot (25g), chopped finely
1 medium tomato (150g), seeded, chopped finely
1 teaspoon finely chopped fresh flat-leaf parsley
12 oysters, on the half shell

1 Place vinegar, oil, shallot, tomato and parsley in screw-top jar; shake well.
2 Top oysters with vinaigrette.

prep time 10 minutes **serves** 2
nutritional count per serving 11.3g total fat (2.1g saturated fat); 652kJ (156 cal); 1.6g carbohydrate; 11.5g protein; 0.7g fibre
tip Make sure the oysters you buy are freshly shucked.

Scallops with saffron cream

12 scallops in half shell (480g)
1 teaspoon olive oil
1 small brown onion (80g), chopped finely
2 teaspoons finely grated lemon rind
pinch saffron threads
⅔ cup (160ml) pouring cream
1 tablespoon lemon juice
2 teaspoons salmon roe

1 Remove scallops from shells; wash and dry shells. Place shells, in single layer, on serving platter.
2 Rinse scallops under cold water; discard scallop roe. Gently pat scallops dry with absorbent paper.
3 Heat oil in small saucepan; cook onion, stirring, until softened. Add rind, saffron and cream; bring to the boil. Reduce heat; simmer, uncovered, about 5 minutes or until mixture has reduced to about ½ cup. Cool 30 minutes. Stir in juice; stand 10 minutes. Strain cream mixture into small bowl then back into same cleaned pan; stir over low heat until heated through.
4 Meanwhile, cook scallops, in batches, on heated oiled grill plate (or grill or barbecue) until browned and cooked as desired.
5 Return scallops to shells; top with cream sauce and roe.

prep + cook time 15 minutes (+ cooling) **makes** 12
nutritional count per scallop 6.4g total fat (4g saturated fat); 288kJ (69 cal); 0.8g carbohydrate; 2.3g protein; 0.1g fibre

Entrées

Onion soup with gruyère croûtons

50g (1½ pounds) butter
4 large brown onions (800g), sliced thinly
¾ cup (180ml) dry white wine
3 cups (750ml) water
1 litre (4 cups) beef stock
1 dried bay leaf
1 tablespoon plain (all-purpose) flour
1 teaspoon fresh thyme leaves

gruyère croûtons
1 small french bread stick (150g), cut in 2cm (¾-inch) slices
½ cup (60g) coarsely grated gruyère cheese

1 Melt butter in large saucepan; cook onion, stirring occasionally, about 30 minutes or until caramelised.
2 Meanwhile, bring wine to the boil in large saucepan; boil 1 minute then stir in the water, stock and bay leaf. Return to the boil. Remove from heat.
3 Stir flour into onion mixture; cook, stirring, 2 minutes. Gradually add hot broth mixture to onion mixture; cook, stirring, until mixture boils and thickens slightly. Reduce heat; simmer, uncovered, stirring occasionally, 20 minutes. Discard bay leaf; stir in thyme, season to taste.
4 Meanwhile, make gruyère croûtons.
5 Serve bowls of soup topped with croûtons. Sprinkle with extra thyme leaves, if you like.
gruyère croûtons Preheat grill (broiler). Toast bread on one side then turn and sprinkle with cheese; grill croûtons until cheese browns lightly.

prep + cook time 1 hour 10 minutes **serves** 4
nutritional count per serving 16.7g total fat (10g saturated fat); 1522kJ (364 cal); 31.1g carbohydrate; 13.4g protein; 3.9g fibre
tip This recipe is not suitable to freeze.

Chicken, pea and asparagus soup with pistou

3 cups (750ml) chicken stock
3 cups (750ml) water
1 clove garlic, crushed
¼ teaspoon coarsely ground black pepper
400g (12½ ounces) chicken breast fillets
170g (5½ ounces) asparagus, trimmed, chopped coarsely
1½ cups (240g) shelled fresh peas
1 tablespoon lemon juice
pistou
1 cup coarsely chopped fresh basil
2 teaspoons finely grated lemon rind
1 clove garlic, crushed
2 teaspoons olive oil

1 Bring stock, the water, garlic and pepper to the boil in large saucepan. Add chicken; return to the boil. Reduce heat; simmer, covered, about 10 minutes or until chicken is cooked through. Cool in poaching liquid 10 minutes. Remove chicken from pan; slice thinly.
2 Meanwhile, make pistou.
3 Add remaining ingredients to soup; bring to the boil. Return chicken to pan; simmer, uncovered, about 3 minutes or until vegetables are just tender.
4 Serve bowls of soup topped with pistou.
pistou Using mortar and pestle, pound all ingredients until smooth.

prep + cook time 30 minutes **serves** 4
nutritional count per serving 5.7g total fat (1.3g saturated fat); 861kJ (206 cal); 7.3g carbohydrate; 28.9g protein; 4.4g fibre
tip You will need 450g (14½ ounces) of fresh peas in the pod or 2 cups (240g) frozen peas for this recipe.

Potato and leek soup

2 medium potatoes (400g), chopped coarsely
2 medium carrots (240g), chopped coarsely
1 large brown onion (200g), chopped coarsely
1 medium tomato (150g), chopped coarsely
1 stalk celery (150g), trimmed, chopped coarsely
1.5 litres (6 cups) water
1 tablespoon olive oil
50g (1½ ounces) butter
4 medium potatoes (800g), chopped coarsely, extra
1 large leek (500g), sliced thickly
1¼ cups (310ml) pouring cream
2 tablespoons finely chopped fresh chives
1 tablespoon each finely chopped fresh basil and dill
croûtons
2 slices wholemeal bread (90g)
50g (1½ ounces) butter

1 Combine potato, carrot, onion, tomato, celery and the water in large saucepan; bring to the boil. Reduce heat; simmer, uncovered, 20 minutes. Strain broth through muslin-lined sieve or colander into large heatproof bowl; discard solids.
2 Heat oil and butter in same cleaned pan; cook extra potato and leek, covered, 15 minutes, stirring occasionally. Add broth; bring to the boil. Reduce heat; simmer, covered, 15 minutes. Stand 10 minutes.
3 Meanwhile, make croûtons.
4 Blend or process soup, in batches, until smooth. Return soup to same cleaned pan; stir in cream over medium heat until hot.
5 Serve bowls of soup sprinkled with combined herbs, topped with croûtons.
croûtons Cut and discard crusts from bread; cut into 1cm (½-inch) pieces. Melt butter in medium frying pan, add bread; cook, stirring, until browned. Drain on absorbent paper.

prep + cook time 1 hour 25 minutes **serves** 4
nutritional count per serving 47.9g total fat (28.8g saturated fat); 2822kJ (675 cal); 46.3g carbohydrate; 11g protein; 9.8g fibre
nutritional count per serving of croûtons 10.7g total fat (6.8g saturated fat); 535kJ (128 cal); 6.2g carbohydrate; 1.6g protein; 1g fibre
tip It is fine to use just one 300ml carton of cream in this recipe.

Creamy watercress soup

1 tablespoon olive oil
1 small brown onion (80g), chopped finely
1 small leek (200g), sliced thinly
3 medium potatoes (600g), chopped coarsely
1 litre (4 cups) chicken stock
3 cups (350g) firmly packed trimmed watercress
⅓ cup (80g) sour cream

1 Heat oil in large saucepan; cook onion and leek, stirring over low heat, until vegetables soften. Add potato and stock; bring to the boil. Reduce heat; simmer, covered, about 20 minutes or until potato is almost tender.
2 Reserve four watercress sprigs; stir remaining watercress into pan. Simmer soup, uncovered, about 5 minutes or until potato is tender. Stand 10 minutes.
3 Blend or process soup, in batches, until smooth. Return soup to same cleaned pan; stir until heated through.
4 Serve bowls of soup topped with sour cream and reserved watercress.

prep + cook time 1 hour **serves** 4
nutritional count per serving 13.3g total fat (6.1g saturated fat); 1091kJ (261 cal); 22.9g carbohydrate; 9.5g protein; 6.4g fibre
tips Watercress is from the cress family. It has a peppery taste and is very popular in France. It is also served in salads and as a garnish for grilled steaks. It is highly perishable, so should be used as soon as possible after purchase.

Cream of chicken soup

1.8kg (3½-pound) whole chicken
1 medium carrot (120g), chopped coarsely
1 stalk celery (150g), trimmed, chopped coarsely
1 medium brown onion (150g), chopped coarsely
2 litres (8 cups) water
1 litre (4 cups) chicken stock
40g (1½ ounces) butter
⅓ cup (50g) plain (all-purpose) flour
2 tablespoons lemon juice
½ cup (125ml) pouring cream
¼ cup finely chopped fresh flat-leaf parsley

1 Place chicken, carrot, celery and onion in large saucepan, add the water and stock; bring to the boil. Reduce heat; simmer, covered, 1½ hours. Remove chicken from pan; simmer broth, covered, 30 minutes.
2 Strain broth through muslin-lined sieve or colander into large heatproof bowl; discard solids.
3 Melt butter in large saucepan, add flour; cook, stirring, until mixture thickens and bubbles. Gradually stir in broth and juice; stir over heat until mixture boils and thickens slightly. Add cream, reduce heat; simmer, uncovered, about 25 minutes, stirring occasionally.
4 Meanwhile, remove and discard skin and bones from chicken; shred meat coarsely.
5 Add chicken to soup; stir over medium heat until hot. Serve bowls of soup sprinkled with parsley.

prep + cook time 3 hours **serves** 4
nutritional count per serving 59.2g total fat (26.2g saturated fat); 3327kJ (796 cal); 15.7g carbohydrate; 50.7g protein; 2.5g fibre
serving suggestion Slices of crusty bread.

Vichyssoise

30g (1 ounce) butter
1 large brown onion (200g), chopped finely
1 large leek (500g), sliced thickly
4 medium potatoes (800g), chopped coarsely
1.5 litres (6 cups) chicken stock
1¼ cups (310ml) pouring cream
2 tablespoons finely chopped fresh chives

1 Melt butter in large saucepan; cook onion and leek, stirring, about 10 minutes or until soft. Add potato and stock; bring to the boil. Reduce heat; simmer, covered, 15 minutes. Stand 10 minutes.
2 Blend or process soup, in batches, until smooth. Stir cream into soup; cover, refrigerate 3 hours or overnight.
3 Serve bowls of soup sprinkled with chives.

prep + cook time 45 minutes (+ refrigeration) **serves** 4
nutritional count per serving 40.6g total fat (26.3g saturated fat); 2299kJ (550 cal); 32.8g carbohydrate; 12g protein; 5.6g fibre
tips Vichyssoise (pronounced vish-ee-swaz) is a cold soup made with potatoes and leeks. Use only the white part of the leeks in this recipe to preserve the creamy whiteness of the soup.
It is fine to use just one 300ml carton of cream in this recipe.

Melon in prosciutto

1 small rockmelon (1.3kg), halved lengthways
12 thin slices prosciutto (180g)
2 tablespoons extra virgin olive oil
¼ cup loosely packed fresh flat-leaf parsley leaves

1 Peel and seed rockmelon; cut into 12 wedges.
2 Wrap one prosciutto slice around each melon wedge, place on serving platter; drizzle with oil, sprinkle with parsley.

prep time 20 minutes **serves** 4
nutritional count per serving 11.9g total fat (2.2g saturated fat); 802kJ (192 cal); 10.9g carbohydrate; 9.4g protein; 2.5g fibre
tip We have used prosciutto but France also produces salted, air-cured and aged ham called "jambon de pays" or "jambon de Bayonne" if it's from the south west Basque region.

Shallot and blue cheese tartlets

1 ½ cups (225g) plain (all-purpose) flour
125g (4 ounces) cold butter, chopped coarsely
2 egg yolks
1 tablespoon water, approximately
1 egg white, beaten lightly
filling
60g (2 ounces) butter
250g (8 ounces) shallots, chopped finely
3 eggs, beaten lightly
1 ¼ cups (310ml) pouring cream
30g (1 ounce) blue cheese

1 Sift flour into bowl, rub in butter. Add egg yolks and enough water to make ingredients cling together. Press dough into a ball, cover; refrigerate 30 minutes.
2 Preheat oven to 200°C/400°F.
3 Roll pastry until large enough to line six 11cm (4-inch) flan tins. Place tins on oven tray; prick pastry all over with fork. Line pastry with baking paper, fill with dried beans or rice. Bake 10 minutes. Remove paper and beans; bake further 5 minutes or until browned. Brush sides and bases with egg white; cool.
4 Reduce oven to 180°C/350°F.
5 Meanwhile, make filling; pour into cases.
6 Bake tartlets about 15 minutes or until filling is set.
filling Melt butter in frying pan; cook shallots, stirring constantly, until soft. Drain on absorbent paper; cool. Combine egg, cream, crumbled cheese and shallot mixture in medium bowl.

prep + cook time 45 minutes (+ refrigeration & cooling) **makes** 6
nutritional count per tartlet 54.3g total fat (34g saturated fat); 2721kJ (651 cal); 29.9g carbohydrate; 11.7g protein; 1.8g fibre
tip It is fine to use just one 300ml carton of cream in this recipe.

Caramelised onion and goat's cheese tartlets

1 cup (150g) plain (all-purpose) flour
80g (2½ ounces) cold butter, chopped coarsely
1 egg yolk
2 tablespoons iced water, approximately
100g (3 ounces) soft goat's cheese
2 tablespoons coarsely chopped fresh chives
caramelised onion
2 tablespoons olive oil
4 large brown onions (800g), sliced thinly
⅓ cup (80ml) port
2 tablespoons red wine vinegar
2 tablespoons light brown sugar

1 Process flour and butter until crumbly. Add egg yolk and enough of the water to process until ingredients come together. Enclose in plastic wrap; refrigerate 30 minutes.
2 Meanwhile, make caramelised onion.
3 Preheat oven to 200°C/400°F. Grease four 10.5cm (4-inch) loose-based flan tins.
4 Divide pastry into four portions. Roll each portion of pastry between sheets of baking paper until large enough to line tins. Lift pastry into tins, press into base and side; trim edge, prick base all over with fork.
5 Place tins on oven tray; line pastry with baking paper, fill with dried beans or rice. Bake 10 minutes. Remove paper and beans; bake further 5 minutes or until tartlet shells brown lightly.
6 Divide onion mixture and cheese among tartlets. Bake about 5 minutes or until heated through. Sprinkle tartlets with chives.
caramelised onion Heat oil in large frying pan; cook onion, stirring, until onion softens. Add port, vinegar and sugar; cook, stirring occasionally, about 25 minutes or until onion caramelises.

prep + cook time 1 hour (+ refrigeration) **makes** 4
nutritional count per tartlet 31.5g total fat (15.2g saturated fat); 2165kJ (518 cal); 43.6g carbohydrate; 11g protein; 4g fibre
tip It's surprising how long it takes to caramelise onions. The time we give is only a guide – longer, slower cooking time will give the best results.

Tomato, olive and goat's cheese tart

2 sheets puff pastry
¾ cup (110g) semi-dried tomatoes, chopped
¾ cup (90g) seeded black olives
½ cup (120g) soft goat's cheese, crumbled
½ small red onion (50g), sliced
¼ cup fresh torn basil leaves
1 egg, beaten lightly

1 Preheat oven to 200°C/400°F. Line oven tray with baking paper.
2 Cut a 16cm x 24cm (6-inch x 9½-inch) rectangle from one pastry sheet; place on oven tray. Top with tomato, olives, cheese, onion and basil leaves.
3 Cut a 18cm x 24cm (7-inch x 9½-inch) rectangle from remaining pastry sheet; score pastry in a diamond pattern then place on top of filling, press edges to seal. Brush with egg.
4 Bake tart about 20 minutes.

prep + cook time 30 minutes **serves** 4
nutritional count per serving 26.4g total fat (5.1g saturated fat); 2036kJ (487 cal); 45.7g carbohydrate; 13.7g protein; 5.7g fibre
tip Goat's cheese is very popular in France. There are over a hundred different types of goat's cheeses produced.

Caramelised fennel tarts

50g (1 ½ ounces) butter
4 baby fennel bulbs (520g), trimmed, halved lengthways
1 teaspoon finely grated orange rind
½ cup (125ml) orange juice
1 sheet puff pastry
2 teaspoons finely chopped fresh thyme

1 Preheat oven to 220°C/425°F. Oil and line two oven trays.
2 Melt butter in large frying pan; cook fennel until browned lightly. Add rind and juice; bring to the boil. Reduce heat; simmer, uncovered, about 5 minutes or until fennel is caramelised and tender.
3 Cut pastry sheet into four squares; place on oven trays. Remove fennel from pan, leaving behind the pan juices; divide among pastry squares.
4 Bake tarts about 20 minutes or until pastry is browned.
5 Meanwhile, return pan juices to the boil. Reduce heat; simmer, uncovered, until sauce thickens slightly.
6 Serve tarts drizzled with sauce and sprinkled with thyme.

prep + cook time 45 minutes **serves** 4
nutritional count per serving 19.8g total fat (11.9g saturated fat); 1145kJ (274 cal); 19.9g carbohydrate; 3.3g protein; 2.7g fibre

Asparagus hollandaise

1kg (2 pounds) asparagus, trimmed
hollandaise sauce
2 tablespoons water
2 tablespoons white wine vinegar
¼ teaspoon cracked black pepper
2 egg yolks
200g (6½ ounces) unsalted butter, melted

1 Make hollandaise sauce.
2 Boil, steam or microwave asparagus until tender.
3 Serve asparagus on a large platter drizzled with sauce.
hollandaise sauce Bring the water, vinegar and pepper to the boil in small saucepan. Reduce heat; simmer, uncovered, until liquid is reduced to 1 tablespoon. Strain mixture through fine sieve into medium heatproof bowl; cool 10 minutes. Whisk egg yolks into vinegar mixture. Set bowl over medium saucepan of simmering water; do not allow water to touch base of bowl. Whisk mixture over heat until thickened. Remove bowl from heat; gradually whisk in melted butter in a thin, steady stream, whisking constantly until sauce is thick and creamy.

prep + cook time 35 minutes **serves** 4
nutritional count per serving 44g total fat (26.9g saturated fat); 1797kJ (430 cal); 2.8g carbohydrate; 6.1g protein; 2.6g fibre

Herb omelette (fines herbes omelette)

12 eggs
2 tablespoons each finely chopped fresh flat-leaf parsley, chervil and chives
1 tablespoon finely chopped fresh tarragon
⅓ cup (80ml) water
20g (¾ ounce) butter
1 tablespoon olive oil

1 Lightly whisk eggs, herbs and the water in large bowl until just combined.
2 Heat a quarter of the butter and 1 teaspoon of the oil in small omelette pan. When butter is just bubbling, add a quarter of the egg mixture; tilt pan to cover base with egg mixture. Cook over medium heat until omelette is just set. Use a spatula to lift and fold omelette in half; cook further 30 seconds. Carefully slide omelette onto serving plate.
3 Repeat with remaining butter, oil and egg mixture (wiping out the pan after each omelette), to make a total of four omelettes. Serve immediately.

prep + cook time 20 minutes **serves** 4
nutritional count per serving 24.4g total fat (8.2g saturated fat); 1254kJ (300 cal); 0.6g carbohydrate; 20.1g protein; 0.2g fibre
tips Be careful not to overbeat the eggs as it will make the omelette tough. Using a mixture of butter and oil to cook the omelette stops the butter from burning.

Gruyère soufflé

⅓ cup (50g) plain (all-purpose) flour
1⅔ cups (410ml) milk
20g (¾ ounce) butter, chopped
6 eggs, separated
1⅓ cups (165g) grated gruyère cheese
90g (3 ounces) sliced smoked salmon
1½ teaspoons drained baby capers, rinsed
1 tablespoon fresh chervil leaves

1 Preheat oven to 200°C/400°F. Grease 2-litre (8-cup) ovenproof soufflé dish; place on oven tray.
2 Place flour in small saucepan; gradually whisk in milk to form a smooth paste. Cook flour mixture over medium heat, whisking constantly, until mixture boils and thickens. Remove from heat; stir in butter. Whisk in egg yolks and cheese; transfer mixture to large bowl.
3 Beat egg whites in large bowl with electric mixer until soft peaks form. Fold egg white into cheese mixture, in two batches. Pour mixture into dish.
4 Bake soufflé about 35 minutes or until well risen and browned.
5 Meanwhile, arrange salmon on serving platter, top with capers and chervil.
6 Serve soufflé immediately with salmon.

prep + cook time 55 minutes **serves** 4
nutritional count per serving 29.6g total fat (15.8g saturated fat); 1881kJ (450 cal); 14.4g carbohydrate; 31.7g protein; 0.5g fibre
tip Soufflé must be made just before serving.

Goat's cheese soufflé

cooking-oil spray
¼ cup (25g) packaged breadcrumbs
30g (1 ounce) butter
2 tablespoons plain (all-purpose) flour
1 cup (250ml) milk
4 eggs, separated
¼ teaspoon cayenne pepper
150g (4½ ounces) firm goat's cheese, crumbled
creamed spinach sauce
180g (5½ ounces) baby spinach leaves
⅔ cup (160ml) pouring cream, warmed

1 Preheat oven to 200°C/400°F. Spray six 1-cup (250ml) soufflé dishes with cooking-oil spray, sprinkle with breadcrumbs; place on oven tray.
2 Melt butter in small saucepan, add flour; cook, stirring, until mixture bubbles and thickens. Gradually add milk, stirring until mixture boils and thickens. Transfer to large bowl; stir in egg yolks, pepper and cheese. Cool 5 minutes.
3 Beat egg whites in small bowl with electric mixer until soft peaks form. Fold egg white into cheese mixture, in two batches. Spoon mixture into dishes.
4 Bake soufflés about 15 minutes or until puffed and browned lightly.
5 Meanwhile, make creamed spinach sauce.
6 Serve soufflés with sauce.
creamed spinach sauce Boil, steam or microwave spinach until just wilted; drain. When cool enough to handle, squeeze out excess liquid. Blend or process spinach until almost smooth. With motor operating, gradually add cream; process until smooth.

prep + cook time 40 minutes (+ cooling) **serves** 6
nutritional count per serving 26g total fat (15.2g saturated fat); 1315kJ (314 cal); 8.8g carbohydrate; 11.4g protein; 1.1g fibre
tip Soufflé must be made just before serving.

Scallops with fennel and pernod sauce

24 scallops, on the half shell (600g)
60g (2 ounces) butter
2 medium fennel bulbs (600g), trimmed, sliced thinly
4 green onions (scallions), sliced thinly
⅓ cup (80ml) pernod
1¼ cups (310ml) pouring cream
1 tablespoon coarsely chopped fennel frond tips, for serving

1 Remove scallops from shells; wash shells, dry thoroughly, reserve.
2 Melt two-thirds of the butter in large frying pan; cook fennel, in batches, stirring occasionally, about 20 minutes or until softened. Remove from pan.
3 Heat remaining butter in same pan; cook onion, stirring, until soft. Return fennel to pan with scallops, pernod and cream; cook about 2 minutes or until scallops are opaque.
4 Divide shells among serving plates. Using slotted spoon, transfer scallops to shells. Reduce heat under sauce; simmer, stirring, until sauce thickens slightly. Spoon sauce over scallops; sprinkle with frond tips.

prep + cook time 50 minutes **serves** 6
nutritional count per serving 30.9g total fat (20.2g saturated fat); 1563kJ (374 cal); 10.3g carbohydrate; 6.1g protein; 1.7g fibre
tips Pernod is an anise-flavoured liqueur drunk straight, or diluted with ice or water, as an aperitif. The French also call it pastis, and it is a very popular drink consumed in late afternoon as an appetite stimulant.
When trimming the fennel bulbs, keep in mind you will need 1 tablespoon of frond tips to sprinkle on the scallops before serving.
It is fine to use just one 300ml carton of cream in this recipe.

Tuna tartare

200g (6½ ounces) piece sashimi tuna, trimmed
1 tablespoon drained capers, rinsed, chopped finely
2 teaspoons prepared horseradish
⅓ cup (80ml) lime juice
2 small tomatoes (180g), seeded, chopped finely
1 small avocado (200g), chopped finely
1 small red onion (100g), chopped finely
1 baby cos lettuce, trimmed, leaves separated
1 tablespoon extra virgin olive oil

1 Cut tuna into 5mm (¼-inch) pieces. Place tuna in medium bowl with capers, horseradish and 1 tablespoon of the juice; toss to combine. Cover; refrigerate 30 minutes.
2 Combine tomato, avocado, onion and remaining juice in another medium bowl.
3 Serve lettuce leaves topped with tomato mixture and tuna tartare; drizzle with oil.

prep time 25 minutes (+ refrigeration) **serves** 6
nutritional count per serving 10.4g total fat (2.3g saturated fat); 610kJ (146 cal); 2.4g carbohydrate; 9.8g protein; 1.6g fibre
tips Tuna sold as sashimi has to meet stringent guidelines regarding its handling and treatment after leaving the water, but it is still probably a good idea to buy it only from a fishmonger you trust or to seek advice from local authorities before eating any raw seafood.
Horseradish is sold in various forms; make sure you use the prepared white horseradish version in this recipe and not horseradish cream.

Smoked salmon with capers

320g (10 ounces) sliced smoked salmon
1 small red onion (100g), chopped finely
½ cup (90g) drained baby capers, rinsed
2 small witlof (belgian endive) (110g), leaves separated
2 red radishes (70g), trimmed, sliced thinly
1 baby fennel bulb (130g), sliced thinly
mustard honey dressing
1 teaspoon dijon mustard
2 teaspoons honey
2 tablespoons lemon juice
1 tablespoon finely chopped fresh dill
¼ cup (60ml) olive oil

1 Make mustard honey dressing.
2 Divide salmon among serving plates; sprinkle with onion and capers.
3 Serve salmon with witlof, radish and fennel; drizzle with dressing.
mustard honey dressing Place ingredients in screw-top jar; shake well. Season to taste.

prep + cook time 25 minutes **serves** 8
nutritional count per serving 8.8g total fat (1.3g saturated fat); 564kJ (135 cal); 3.7g carbohydrate; 9.8g protein; 1g fibre

Artichoke hearts vinaigrette

1 medium lemon (140g), chopped coarsely
20 small globe artichokes (2kg)
2 cups (500ml) dry white wine
¼ cup loosely packed fresh thyme leaves
5 cloves garlic, unpeeled
½ cup (125ml) lemon juice
2 teaspoons sea salt flakes
1 cup (250ml) white wine vinegar
2 cups (500ml) water
1 tablespoon extra virgin olive oil

1 Place lemon in large bowl half-filled with water. Discard outer leaves from artichokes; cut tips from remaining leaves. Trim, then peel stalks; place artichokes in lemon water.
2 Cut a piece of baking paper into a round to fit inside a large saucepan.
3 Place wine, thyme, garlic, juice, salt, vinegar, the water and drained artichokes in large saucepan; cover with baking-paper round. Bring to the boil. Reduce heat; simmer, covered, about 25 minutes or until artichokes are tender. Cool in poaching liquid about 30 minutes.
4 Whisk ½ cup of the poaching liquid in small bowl with oil (discard remaining liquid).
5 Halve artichokes lengthways; using small knife, remove chokes. Divide artichokes among serving bowls; drizzle with poaching mixture.

prep + cook time 1 hour 30 minutes (+ cooling) **serves** 4
nutritional count per serving 5.5g total fat (0.7g saturated fat); 865kJ (207 cal); 6.7g carbohydrate; 10.4g protein; 4.4g fibre
serving suggestion Sprinkle with extra thyme leaves and serve with crusty bread.

Marinated duck with peppered strawberries

¾ cup (225g) rock salt
¾ cup (165g) firmly packed light brown sugar
2 tablespoons sichuan pepper
4 duck breasts (880g)
70g (2½ ounces) baby rocket (arugula) leaves
peppered strawberries
250g (8 ounces) strawberries, hulled, halved
½ teaspoon ground white pepper
½ teaspoon finely cracked black pepper
¼ cup (60ml) olive oil
1½ cups (225g) cherries, seeded, halved
2 tablespoons balsamic vinegar
1 tablespoon finely grated orange rind
2 tablespoons orange juice
2 shallots (50g), chopped finely

1 Combine rock salt, sugar and pepper in large bowl, add duck breasts; turn to coat. Cover; refrigerate 3 hours.
2 Brush off marinade; pat duck dry with absorbent paper. Place duck, skin-side down, in oiled heated large frying pan; cook, over low heat, about 20 minutes or until skin is browned. Turn duck; cook about 4 minutes or until cooked to your liking. Remove duck from pan, cover loosely with foil; stand 10 minutes before slicing thickly.
3 Meanwhile, make peppered strawberries.
4 Serve duck on rocket with strawberries.
peppered strawberries Combine strawberries, peppers and 1 tablespoon of the oil in medium bowl. Cook strawberry mixture on hot grill plate (or barbecue) for 30 seconds. Transfer to medium bowl; cool. Stir in cherries, vinegar, rind, juice, shallot and remaining oil.

prep + cook time 45 minutes (+ refrigeration) **serves** 6
nutritional count per serving 63.4g total fat (17.9g saturated fat); 3252kJ (778 cal); 33.4g carbohydrate; 20.7g protein; 1.9g fibre
tip Duck breasts are available from poultry shops and some butcher shops.

Chicken with tarragon cream

8 chicken drumettes (560g)
8 chicken wingettes (440g)
1 medium red onion (170g), chopped finely
1 clove garlic, crushed
1 bay leaf
½ cup (125ml) dry white wine
½ cup (125ml) water

tarragon cream

¼ cup (60g) cream cheese, softened
1 tablespoon coarsely chopped fresh tarragon
1 tablespoon lemon juice
¼ cup (75g) mayonnaise
2 tablespoons warm water

1 Make tarragon cream.
2 Cook chicken, in batches, in heated oiled large frying pan until browned.
3 Return chicken to pan; stir in onion, garlic and bay leaf then wine. Bring to the boil; boil, uncovered, 2 minutes. Add the water; bring to the boil. Reduce heat; simmer, uncovered, until liquid is almost evaporated and chicken is cooked. Cool.
4 Serve chicken with tarragon cream.
tarragon cream Beat cream cheese until smooth; stir in remaining ingredients.

prep + cook time 25 minutes **serves** 8
nutritional count per serving 11.7g total fat (3.9g saturated fat); 1003kJ (240 cal); 3.4g carbohydrate; 27.6g protein; 0.4g fibre
tip If you can't find drumettes and wingettes, buy eight chicken wings; chop off and discard the tips from wings, then chop the remaining pieces in half at the joint.

BISTROT
BRASSERIE

Coquilles saint jacques

1½ cups (375ml) chicken stock
1 cup (250ml) dry white wine
2 shallots (50g), chopped finely
750g (1½ pounds) scallops, without roe
250g (8 ounces) button mushrooms, sliced thinly
45g (1½ ounces) butter
2 tablespoons plain (all-purpose) flour
½ cup (125ml) milk
½ cup (125ml) pouring cream
2 egg yolks
2 teaspoons lemon juice
1 cup (70g) stale breadcrumbs
2 tablespoons finely grated gruyère cheese
1 tablespoon finely chopped fresh chives
30g (1 ounce) butter, melted, extra

1 Bring stock, wine and shallots to the boil in medium saucepan; reduce heat. Add scallops and mushrooms; simmer 2 minutes or until scallops are barely cooked. Using slotted spoon, remove scallops and mushrooms.
2 Bring poaching liquid to the boil; boil 5 minutes or until reduced to ½ cup. Strain into heatproof bowl; reserve liquid.
3 Melt butter in small saucepan, add flour; cook, stirring, until mixture bubbles and thickens. Gradually stir in combined milk, cream and reserved poaching liquid; cook, stirring, until mixture boils and thickens. Remove from heat; whisk in egg yolks and juice.
4 Preheat grill (broiler).
5 Combine breadcrumbs, cheese, chives and extra butter in medium bowl. Divide scallops and mushrooms among four 1-cup (250ml) gratin dishes; spoon over sauce. Sprinkle with breadcrumb mixture. Place scallops under grill until browned lightly.

prep + cook time 45 minutes **serves** 4
nutritional count per serving 38.8g total fat (23.5g saturated fat); 2558kJ (612 cal); 21.1g carbohydrate; 33.9g protein; 2.7g fibre
tip Look for fresh scallops as frozen scallops give out a lot of water.

Mains

Roast loin of pork with apple sauce

2.5kg (5-pound) boneless loin of pork, rind on
2 sprigs rosemary
1 tablespoon olive oil
1 tablespoon coarse cooking (kosher) salt
apple sauce
3 large apples (600g)
¼ cup (60ml) water
1 teaspoon white sugar
pinch ground cinnamon

1 Preheat oven to 240°C/475°F.
2 Using sharp knife, score pork rind by making shallow cuts at 1cm (½-inch) intervals. Tie pork at 2cm (¾-inch) intervals with kitchen string; tuck rosemary under string. Place pork in large baking dish; rub with oil, then salt. Roast about 40 minutes or until rind blisters. Drain excess fat from dish.
3 Reduce oven to 180°C/350°F; roast pork about 1 hour. Transfer pork to plate; cover loosely, stand 15 minutes before carving.
4 Meanwhile, make apple sauce.
5 Serve pork with apple sauce.
apple sauce Peel and core apples; slice thickly. Place apples and the water in medium saucepan; simmer, uncovered, about 10 minutes or until apple is soft. Remove pan from heat; stir in sugar and cinnamon.

prep + cook time 2 hours **serves** 8
nutritional count per serving 72g total fat (24.1g saturated fat); 3762kJ (900 cal); 7.7g carbohydrate; 56.7g protein; 1.1g fibre
tip Ask your butcher to roll and tie the pork at 2cm (¾-inch) intervals for you, and to score the rind, if it isn't already done.

Pot au feu with stuffed cabbage rolls

2 veal shanks (1.5kg)
2 large carrots (360g), chopped coarsely
1 medium leek (350g), chopped coarsely
2 small turnips (300g), chopped coarsely
6 baby onions (150g)
1 bay leaf
3 cups (750ml) chicken stock
1 litre (4 cups) water
1 small savoy cabbage (1.2kg)
250g (8 ounces) minced (ground) pork
250g (8 ounces) minced (ground) chicken
1 egg
1 small brown onion (80g), chopped finely
½ cup (50g) packaged breadcrumbs

1 Place veal, carrot, leek, turnip, whole onions, bay leaf, stock and the water in large saucepan; bring to the boil. Reduce heat; simmer, uncovered, about 1½ hours or until veal is tender. Remove veal; when cool enough to handle, remove meat from bones and chop coarsely.
2 Remove 12 large leaves from cabbage; cook, uncovered, in batches, in large saucepan of boiling water 3 minutes. Drain leaves on absorbent paper. Finely chop enough of the remaining cabbage to make ⅓ cup; reserve remaining cabbage for another use.
3 Meanwhile, using hand combine pork, chicken, egg, onion, breadcrumbs and chopped cabbage in large bowl; divide mixture among cabbage leaves. Roll leaves to enclose filling, secure with toothpicks.
4 Return veal meat to vegetable mixture in pan, add cabbage rolls; bring to the boil. Reduce heat; simmer, uncovered, about 10 minutes or until cabbage rolls are cooked through.
5 Divide cabbage rolls among serving bowls; ladle soup over top.

prep + cook time 2 hours 30 minutes **serves** 6
nutritional count per serving 8.6g total fat (2.7g saturated fat); 1714kJ (410 cal); 20g carbohydrate; 57.2g protein; 11.7g fibre
tips The literal translation of "pot on the fire" refers to the way this old recipe was originally cooked, in a huge cast-iron pot directly in the fireplace. Any combination of vegetables and meat can be used, and the French versions are as numerous as there are regions of the country. When peeling turnips, make sure you remove all the bitter outer layer.

Fish stew with saffron, tomato and wine

500g (1 pound) uncooked medium king prawns (shrimp)
500g (1 pound) small mussels
1 tablespoon olive oil
1 medium brown onion (150g), chopped finely
3 cloves garlic, crushed
1 small leek (200g), sliced thinly
1 small fennel bulb (200g), sliced thinly
1 stalk celery (150g), trimmed, sliced thinly
½ cup (125ml) dry white wine
800g (1½ pounds) canned diced tomatoes
1 litre (4 cups) fish stock
pinch saffron threads
200g (6½ ounces) kipfler potatoes, cut into 1cm (½-inch) slices
300g (9½ ounces) skinless firm white fish fillet, chopped coarsely
300g (9½ ounces) skinless salmon fillet, chopped coarsely

1 Shell and devein prawns. Scrub mussels; remove beards.
2 Heat oil in large flameproof dish; cook onion, garlic, leek, fennel and celery, stirring, about 10 minutes or until vegetables soften.
3 Add wine, undrained tomatoes, stock, saffron and potato to pan; bring to the boil. Reduce heat; simmer, uncovered, about 10 minutes or until potato is tender.
4 Add prawns and fish to pan; cook, uncovered, 5 minutes. Add mussels; cook, covered, about 2 minutes or until mussels open (discard any that do not).

prep + cook time 1 hour **serves** 6
nutritional count per serving 9g total fat (1.9g saturated fat); 1254kJ (300 cal); 13.5g carbohydrate; 35.4g protein; 4.3g fibre

Steamed mussels in tomato garlic broth

1 tablespoon olive oil
2 shallots (50g), chopped finely
4 cloves garlic, crushed
410g (13 ounces) canned crushed tomatoes
1 cup (250ml) dry white wine
1 teaspoon caster (superfine) sugar
2kg (4 pounds) small black mussels
½ cup coarsely chopped fresh flat-leaf parsley

1 Heat oil in large saucepan; cook shallot and garlic, stirring, until shallot softens.
2 Add undrained tomatoes, wine and sugar; bring to the boil. Reduce heat; simmer, uncovered, about 10 minutes or until sauce thickens slightly.
3 Meanwhile, scrub mussels; remove beards. Add mussels to pan; simmer, covered, about 5 minutes, shaking pan occasionally, until mussels open (discard any that do not). Remove mussels from pan, divide among serving bowls; cover with foil to keep warm.
4 Bring tomato mixture to the boil; boil, uncovered, about 5 minutes or until sauce thickens slightly. Pour tomato mixture over mussels; sprinkle with parsley.

prep + cook time 55 minutes **serves** 4
nutritional count per serving 6.7g total fat (1.2g saturated fat); 828kJ (198 cal); 9.9g carbohydrate; 13.3g protein; 2.2g fibre

Pan-fried freshwater trout with cider and brandy sauce

2 shallots (50g), chopped finely
⅓ cup (80ml) brandy
⅓ cup (80ml) sparkling apple cider
¼ cup (60ml) water
¼ cup (60ml) pouring cream
125g (4 ounces) butter, chopped
¼ cup (35g) plain (all-purpose) flour
1 teaspoon each salt and cracked black pepper
4 freshwater trout fillets (600g), boned
1 tablespoon olive oil
80g (2½ ounces) baby rocket (arugula) leaves

1 Bring shallot, brandy, cider and the water to the boil in medium saucepan. Reduce heat; simmer, uncovered, about 5 minutes or until almost all liquid evaporates.
2 Add cream to pan; simmer, uncovered, 5 minutes. Add butter, a few pieces at a time, whisking to combine between additions. Strain sauce into medium jug; discard solids. Cover to keep warm.
3 Combine flour, salt and pepper in large shallow dish. Coat fish in flour mixture; shake off excess.
4 Heat oil in large frying pan; cook fish until browned lightly and cooked as desired.
5 Divide rocket among serving plates; top with fish, drizzle with sauce.

prep + cook time 55 minutes **serves** 4
nutritional count per serving 42.6g total fat (23.2g saturated fat); 2449kJ (586 cal); 8.7g carbohydrate; 31.2g protein; 0.7g fibre

Seared salmon with leek velouté and salmon roe

3 medium leeks (1kg)
100g (3 ounces) butter
2 tablespoons plain (all-purpose) flour
½ cup (125ml) dry white wine
1 cup (250ml) chicken stock
1 teaspoon dijon mustard
375g (12 ounces) dried egg fettuccine pasta
¼ cup coarsely chopped fresh chervil
1 tablespoon olive oil
6 salmon fillets (1.2kg)
¼ cup (50g) salmon roe

1 Trim cleaned leeks. Cut leeks into 8cm (3¼-inch) lengths; cut lengths in half lengthways, cut halves into thin strips lengthways.
2 Melt all but 1 tablespoon of the butter in large saucepan; cook leek, stirring occasionally, over medium heat, about 15 minutes or until softened. Stir in flour; cook, stirring, 2 minutes. Gradually stir in wine and stock then mustard; stir until velouté boils and thickens. Cover to keep warm.
3 Meanwhile, cook pasta in large saucepan of boiling water until tender; drain. Place pasta in large bowl; stir in chervil and remaining butter.
4 Heat oil in large frying pan; cook fish until browned lightly and cooked as desired.
5 Divide pasta and velouté among serving plates; top with fish and roe.

prep + cook time 1 hour **serves** 6
nutritional count per serving 33g total fat (13g saturated fat); 3056kJ (731 cal); 51.2g carbohydrate; 51.6g protein; 4.7g fibre
tip Velouté, a white sauce made from roux (a cooked butter and flour mixture) and stock, is one of the five "mother" sauces in French cooking from which all other sauces are derived. Its particular charm is that the addition of one or two different ingredients changes its character completely. Classic allemande, bercy, crevettes, normande, supreme, and vin blanc sauces are all based on velouté.

Steamed salmon with burnt orange sauce

½ cup (110g) caster (superfine) sugar
⅓ cup (80ml) water
1 teaspoon finely grated orange rind
¼ cup (60ml) orange juice
1 tablespoon olive oil
1 tablespoon rice wine vinegar
4 salmon fillets (800g)
3 cups (350g) firmly packed trimmed watercress

1 Combine sugar and the water in small saucepan; stir, without boiling, until sugar dissolves. Bring to the boil. Reduce heat; simmer, uncovered, without stirring, until mixture is a light caramel colour.
2 Remove pan from heat; allow bubbles to subside. Carefully stir in rind and juice; return pan to low heat. Stir until any pieces of caramel melt. Remove pan from heat; stir in oil and vinegar.
3 Meanwhile, place fish in large bamboo steamer set over large saucepan of simmering water; steam, covered, 15 minutes.
4 Serve fish with watercress, drizzled with sauce.

prep + cook time 35 minutes **serves** 4
nutritional count per serving 19.1g total fat (3.8g saturated fat); 1940kJ (464 cal); 29.4g carbohydrate; 41.6g protein; 3.4g fibre

Quiche lorraine

1 medium brown onion (150g), chopped finely
3 rindless bacon slices (195g), chopped finely
3 eggs
1¼ cups (310ml) pouring cream
½ cup (125ml) milk
¾ cup (120g) coarsely grated gruyère cheese
pastry
1¾ cups (260g) plain (all-purpose) flour
155g (5 ounces) cold butter, chopped coarsely
1 egg yolk
2 teaspoons lemon juice
⅓ cup (80ml) iced water, approximately

1 Make pastry.
2 Preheat oven to 200°C/400°F.
3 Roll pastry between sheets of baking paper large enough to line a deep 24cm (9½-inch) loose-based fluted flan tin. Lift pastry into tin; gently press pastry around side. Trim edge, place tin on oven tray. Cover pastry with baking paper; fill with dried beans or rice. Bake 10 minutes. Remove paper and beans; bake a further 10 minutes or until golden brown. Cool.
4 Reduce oven to 180°C/350°F.
5 Cook onion and bacon in heated oiled small frying pan until onion is soft; drain on absorbent paper, cool. Sprinkle bacon mixture over pastry case.
6 Whisk eggs in medium bowl then whisk in cream, milk and cheese. Pour mixture into pastry case.
7 Bake quiche about 35 minutes or until filling is set. Stand 5 minutes before removing from tin.
pastry Sift flour into bowl; rub in butter. Add egg yolk, juice and enough water to make ingredients cling together. Knead gently on floured surface until smooth. Cover; refrigerate 30 minutes.

prep + cook time 1 hour 30 minutes (+ refrigeration) **serves** 6
nutritional count per serving 51.8g total fat (35.4g saturated fat); 3139kJ (751 cal); 35.4g carbohydrate; 22.1g protein; 2g fibre
tip It is fine to use just one 300ml carton of cream in this recipe.

Classic onion tart (tarte à l'oignon)

1½ cups (225g) plain (all-purpose) flour
125g (4 ounces) cold butter, chopped coarsely
1 egg yolk
2 tablespoons iced water, approximately
onion filling
60g (2 ounces) butter
1 tablespoon olive oil
5 medium brown onions (750g), sliced thinly
3 egg yolks
½ cup (125ml) pouring cream
pinch ground nutmeg

1 Process flour and butter until mixture is crumbly. Add egg yolk and enough of the water to process until ingredients just come together. Cover; refrigerate 30 minutes.
2 Preheat oven to 200°C/400°F. Grease 22cm (9-inch) round loose-based fluted flan tin.
3 Roll dough between sheets of baking paper until large enough to line tin. Lift pastry into tin, press into base and side, trim edge; prick base all over with fork. Place tin on oven tray; line pastry with baking paper, fill with dried beans or rice. Bake 10 minutes. Remove paper and beans; bake further 10 minutes. Cool.
4 Meanwhile, make onion filling.
5 Reduce oven to 180°C/350°F.
6 Spread onion mixture into tart shell. Bake about 25 minutes or until set.
onion filling Heat butter and oil in large frying pan; cook onion, covered, stirring occasionally, about 30 minutes or until onion is soft. Remove from heat. Add combined egg yolks, cream and nutmeg; mix well. Season to taste.

prep + cook time 1 hour 40 minutes (+ refrigeration & cooling)
serves 8
nutritional count per serving 31.4g total fat (18.2g saturated fat); 1726kJ (413 cal); 25.9g carbohydrate; 6.4g protein; 2.3g fibre

Chicken, mushroom and leek fricassee

2 tablespoons olive oil
1.5kg (3 pounds) chicken thigh fillets, quartered
3 rindless bacon slices (195g), chopped coarsely
45g (1½ ounces) butter
3 medium leeks (1kg), trimmed, sliced thinly
3 stalks celery (450g), trimmed, sliced thinly
3 cloves garlic, crushed
¼ cup loosely packed fresh thyme sprigs
2 bay leaves
2 tablespoons plain (all-purpose) flour
1½ cups (375ml) dry white wine
1½ cups (375ml) chicken stock
400g (13 ounces) button mushrooms
¼ cup (60ml) pouring cream
½ cup coarsely chopped fresh flat-leaf parsley

1 Preheat oven to 160°C/325°F.
2 Heat oil in large heavy-based flameproof dish. Cook chicken, in batches, until browned. Remove from dish.
3 Cook bacon in same dish, stirring, until browned. Add butter and leek; cook, stirring occasionally, until leek softens. Stir in celery, garlic, thyme and bay leaves. Stir in flour, then wine and stock; bring to the boil, stirring.
4 Stir in chicken and mushrooms; transfer to oven. Cook about 20 minutes or until chicken is tender and sauce has thickened slightly.
5 Return dish to stove top, discard bay leaves; stir in cream and parsley. Simmer, uncovered, until heated through.
6 Serve fricassee sprinkled with fresh thyme leaves, if you like.

prep + cook time 50 minutes **serves** 6
nutritional count per serving 39.2g total fat (14.6g saturated fat); 2805kJ (671 cal); 8.6g carbohydrate; 59.1g protein; 6.2g fibre

Lemon and thyme baked chicken

1.5kg (3-pound) whole chicken
1 tablespoon olive oil
1 tablespoon fine salt
2 teaspoons finely cracked black pepper
2 tablespoons fresh thyme leaves
1 bulb garlic, halved crossways
1 medium lemon (140g), cut into wedges
½ bunch fresh thyme sprigs
50g (1½ ounces) butter, softened

1 Preheat oven to 200°C/400°F.
2 Remove and discard any fat from cavity of chicken. Wash chicken under cold water; pat dry inside and out with absorbent paper. Rub chicken with oil. Combine salt, pepper and half the thyme in small bowl; rub onto skin and inside cavity. Place garlic, lemon and thyme sprigs inside cavity.
3 Combine butter and remaining thyme in small bowl. Carefully separate skin from chicken breast with your fingers; spread butter under skin covering breast. Secure skin over cavity with fine skewers or toothpicks.
4 Place chicken on oiled wire rack in shallow roasting pan; roast, uncovered, 1 hour 20 minutes or until chicken is browned and tender. Remove chicken from oven, cover loosely with foil; stand 10 minutes.

prep + cook time 1 hour 45 minutes (+ standing) **serves** 4
nutritional count per serving 39.2g total fat (15.1g saturated fat); 2144kJ (513 cal); 1g carbohydrate; 39.4g protein; 1.4g fibre
tip Take care to dry the chicken completely after rinsing. If there is moisture present when you put it in the oven, it will turn to steam which can prevent the skin from turning a lovely golden brown.

Roasted chicken with 40 cloves of garlic

3 bulbs garlic
60g (2 ounces) butter, softened
1.5kg (3-pound) whole chicken
2 teaspoons salt
2 teaspoons cracked black pepper
1 cup (250ml) water
roasted potatoes
1kg (2 pounds) baby potatoes
cooking-oil spray

1 Preheat oven to 200°C/400°F.
2 Separate cloves from garlic bulb, leaving peel intact. Wash chicken under cold water; pat dry inside and out with absorbent paper. Rub butter over outside of chicken and inside cavity; press combined salt and pepper onto skin and inside cavity. Place half the garlic inside cavity; tie legs together with kitchen string.
3 Place remaining garlic cloves, in single layer, in medium baking dish; place chicken on garlic. Pour the water into dish; roast chicken, uncovered, brushing occasionally with pan juices, about 1 hour 20 minutes or until browned and cooked through.
4 Meanwhile, make roasted potatoes.
5 Stand chicken on platter, loosely covered with foil, 15 minutes.
Serve chicken with roasted garlic and potatoes.
roasted potatoes Boil steam or microwave potatoes 5 minutes; drain. Pat dry with absorbent paper; cool 10 minutes. Place potatoes, in single layer, in large oiled baking dish; spray with cooking-oil spray. Roast potatoes, uncovered, in oven for about the last 30 minutes of chicken cooking time or until potatoes are tender.

prep + cook time 1 hour 40 minutes (+ standing) **serves** 4
nutritional count per serving 45g total fat (17.9g saturated fat); 3219kJ (770 cal); 38.4g carbohydrate; 46.8g protein; 14.1g fibre
tip This moreish Provençal favourite will surprise you with how mild and creamy the garlic becomes after its long roasting. Feel free to use as many cloves as you want because any leftover roasted garlic cloves can be peeled and used to make the simple garlic mayonnaise, aïoli.

Chicken pot roast with mustard cream sauce

1.6kg (3¼-pound) whole chicken
1 tablespoon olive oil
12 shallots (300g), halved
20 baby carrots (400g), trimmed
3 small parsnips (360g), chopped coarsely
1 cup (250ml) dry white wine
2 cups (500ml) chicken stock
2 dried bay leaves
200g (6½ ounces) swiss brown mushrooms
2 tablespoons pouring cream
2 tablespoons wholegrain mustard

1 Preheat oven to 200°C/400°F.
2 Remove and discard any fat from cavity of chicken. Wash chicken under cold water; pat dry inside and out with absorbent paper.
3 Heat oil in large flameproof dish; cook chicken until browned. Remove chicken. Cook shallots, carrots and parsnips in same dish, stirring, about 5 minutes or until vegetables are browned lightly.
4 Return chicken to dish with wine, stock and bay leaves; bring to the boil. Cook, covered, in oven 30 minutes. Uncover; cook about 30 minutes or until chicken is tender. Add mushrooms; cook, uncovered, about 10 minutes or until mushrooms are tender. Remove chicken and vegetables from dish; cover to keep warm.
5 Stir cream and mustard into dish; bring to the boil. Boil, uncovered, about 5 minutes or until sauce thickens slightly.
6 Serve chicken, cut into pieces, with vegetables and sauce.

prep + cook time 2 hours 15 minutes **serves** 4
nutritional count per serving 42.2g total fat (13.8g saturated fat); 2859kJ (684 cal); 16.9g carbohydrate; 46.7g protein; 6.6g fibre

Creamy horseradish chicken with garlic sautéed spinach

1 tablespoon olive oil
4 chicken breast fillets (800g)
1 green onion (scallion), sliced thinly
2 tablespoons dry white wine
⅔ cup (160ml) pouring cream
2 tablespoons prepared horseradish
2 teaspoons lemon juice
½ teaspoon dijon mustard
1 teaspoon finely chopped fresh dill
20g (¾ ounce) butter
2 cloves garlic, crushed
600g (1¼ pounds) trimmed spinach, chopped coarsely

1 Heat half the oil in large frying pan; cook chicken until browned and tender. Remove from pan; cover to keep warm.
2 Heat remaining oil in same pan; cook onion, stirring, until soft. Add wine; bring to the boil. Reduce heat; simmer, uncovered, until liquid is reduced by half. Add cream; bring to the boil. Reduce heat; simmer, uncovered, about 2 minutes or until sauce thickens slightly. Add horseradish, juice, mustard and dill; stir over heat until heated through.
3 Meanwhile, melt butter in large saucepan; cook garlic, stirring, 2 minutes. Add spinach; cook over low heat, covered, 2 minutes or until wilted.
4 Serve chicken and spinach drizzled with sauce.

prep + cook time 30 minutes **serves** 4
nutritional count per serving 38.6g total fat (18.8g saturated fat); 2366kJ (566 cal); 4g carbohydrate; 47.6g protein; 4.6g fibre
tips Horseradish is sold in various forms; make sure you use the prepared white horseradish version in this recipe and not horseradish cream.
You need four large bunches of spinach weighing about 1.6kg (3¼ pounds) to get the amount of trimmed spinach required for this recipe.

Chicken with rosemary and garlic

8 chicken thigh cutlets (1.3kg), skin on
2 tablespoons plain (all-purpose) flour
2 teaspoons sweet paprika
1 teaspoon cracked black pepper
1 tablespoon olive oil
4 cloves garlic, unpeeled
2 stalks fresh rosemary
1½ cups (375ml) chicken stock
½ cup (125ml) dry white wine

1 Preheat oven to 180°C/350°F.
2 Toss chicken in combined flour, paprika and pepper; shake away excess flour mixture.
3 Heat oil in large flameproof baking dish; cook chicken, in batches, until browned. Remove from dish.
4 Return chicken to same dish with garlic, rosemary, stock and wine; bring to the boil. Roast, uncovered, about 40 minutes or until chicken is tender. Remove chicken from dish; cover to keep warm.
5 Cook pan juices in same dish over medium heat, uncovered, about 5 minutes or until sauce thickens slightly.
6 Divide chicken among serving plates, drizzle with sauce.

prep + cook time 1 hour 15 minutes **serves** 4
nutritional count per serving 40.1g total fat (12.4g saturated fat); 2433kJ (582 cal); 5.5g carbohydrate; 43.1g protein; 1.4g fibre
serving suggestion Steamed sugar snap peas.

Chicken and artichoke fricassee

2 tablespoons olive oil
8 chicken drumsticks (1.2kg)
1 medium brown onion (150g), chopped finely
4 cloves garlic, crushed
½ cup (125ml) dry white wine
1½ cups (375ml) chicken stock
1 tablespoon finely grated lemon rind
1 tablespoon lemon juice
1¼ cups (310ml) pouring cream
125g (4 ounces) baby spinach leaves
2 x 340g (11 ounces) jars marinated artichokes in oil, drained, halved
1 tablespoon finely chopped fresh oregano
1 tablespoon fresh oregano leaves

1 Heat half the oil in large saucepan; cook chicken, in batches, until browned. Remove from pan.
2 Heat remaining oil in same pan; cook onion and garlic, stirring, until onion softens. Add wine, stock, rind and juice; bring to the boil. Return chicken to pan; reduce heat, simmer, covered, 20 minutes. Uncover; simmer, about 10 minutes or until chicken is tender.
3 Remove chicken from pan, place two drumsticks in each serving dish.
4 Add cream, spinach, artichokes and chopped oregano to pan with sauce mixture; bring to the boil. Reduce heat; simmer, uncovered, about 2 minutes or until sauce thickens slightly.
5 Pour sauce over chicken; sprinkle with oregano leaves.

prep + cook time 1 hour 10 minutes **serves** 4
nutritional count per serving 65.4g total fat (29.8g saturated fat); 3315kJ (793 cal); 7.4g carbohydrate; 39.4g protein; 2g fibre
tip It is fine to use just one 300ml carton of cream for this recipe.
serving suggestion Serve fricasee with steamed rice.

Caramelised crispy-skin duck

4 duck breast fillets (600g)
¼ cup (55g) light brown sugar
1 teaspoon finely grated orange rind
2 tablespoons orange juice
1 fresh long red chilli, seeded, chopped finely
2cm (¾-inch) piece fresh ginger (10g), grated
1 tablespoon balsamic vinegar

1 Cook duck, skin-side down, in heated large frying pan about 5 minutes or until skin is browned and crisp. Turn duck; cook about 5 minutes or until cooked as desired. Remove from pan; cover to keep warm.
2 Drain all but 2 tablespoons of duck fat from pan; reheat. Add sugar, rind, juice, chilli, ginger and vinegar; bring to the boil. Reduce heat; simmer sauce, uncovered, 2 minutes.
3 Serve duck drizzled with sauce.

prep + cook time 20 minutes **serves** 4
nutritional count per serving 29.1g total fat (8.7g saturated fat); 1868kJ (447 cal); 14.3g carbohydrate; 32.4g protein; 0.1g fibre

Slow-roasted duck with sour cherry sauce

680g (1 ¼ pounds) bottled morello cherries
½ cup (125ml) port
1 cinnamon stick
3 whole cloves
1 clove garlic, sliced thinly
½ cup (125ml) chicken stock
4 duck marylands (1.2kg), excess fat removed

1 Preheat oven to 160°C/325°F.
2 Strain cherries over small bowl; reserve cherries. Combine cherry juice, port, cinnamon, cloves, garlic and stock in large baking dish. Place duck on metal rack in baking dish; cover tightly with oiled foil. Roast, covered, about 2 hours or until duck is tender.
3 Strain pan liquid into medium bowl; skim away fat. Transfer mixture to medium frying pan. Add cherries; bring to the boil. Reduce heat; simmer, uncovered, 5 minutes or until sauce thickens slightly.
4 Serve duck with cherry sauce.

prep + cook time 2 hours 20 minutes **serves** 4
nutritional count per serving 47.3g total fat (12.4g saturated fat); 3156kJ (755 cal); 39.5g carbohydrate; 47.3g protein; 2g fibre
serving suggestion Serve duck with a salad made of apple, roasted walnuts and fresh flat-leaf parsley leaves.

Duck confit with pan-fried kipflers and pear and watercress salad

2 x 2kg (4-pound) whole ducks
1 tablespoon coarse cooking (kosher) salt
2 cloves garlic, sliced thinly
1 bay leaf, crumbled
2 sprigs fresh thyme
2 teaspoons black peppercorns
2 cups (500ml) olive oil
750g (1 ½ pounds) kipfler (fingerling) potatoes, halved lengthways

pear and watercress salad
1 tablespoon wholegrain mustard
1 tablespoon white wine vinegar
1 teaspoon white sugar
¼ cup (60ml) olive oil
3 cups (350g) firmly packed trimmed watercress
1 large pear (330g), sliced thinly

1 Using sharp knife, cut marylands and breasts off ducks. Remove as much fat as possible from carcasses; reserve. Discard wings and carcasses.
2 Combine duck pieces, salt, garlic, bay leaf, thyme and peppercorns in medium bowl. Cover; refrigerate until required.
3 Meanwhile, place reserved fat in large saucepan; cook, uncovered, over low heat, about 1 hour or until fat has melted. Strain mixture through fine sieve into large bowl; discard solids (you will have about 2 cups of duck fat).
4 Preheat oven to 150°C/300°F.
5 Rinse duck pieces under cold water; pat dry with absorbent paper. Place duck pieces, in single layer, in large baking dish. Reserve 2 tablespoons of the fat; pour remaining fat over duck. Top up with olive oil, making sure duck is completely submerged. Roast, uncovered, 2 hours.
6 Boil, steam or microwave potatoes until tender; drain. Heat reserved fat in large frying pan; cook potato, in batches, until browned. Remove from pan; cover to keep warm.
7 Meanwhile, make pear and watercress salad.
8 Place duck in same large frying pan; cook, skin-side down, until skin is crisp. Serve duck with potato and salad.
pear and watercress salad Place mustard, vinegar, sugar and oil in screw-top jar; shake well. Place watercress, pear and dressing in large bowl; toss gently to combine.

prep + cook time 4 hours **serves** 6
nutritional count per serving 184.2g total fat (41.6g saturated fat); 8628kJ (2064 cal); 24.5g carbohydrate; 79.9g protein; 5.5g fibre

Coq au vin

750g (1 ½ pounds) spring onions
¼ cup (60ml) olive oil
6 rindless bacon slices (390g), chopped coarsely
310g (10½ ounces) button mushrooms
2 cloves garlic, crushed
8 chicken thigh fillets (880g)
¼ cup (35g) plain (all-purpose) flour
2 cups (500ml) dry red wine
1 ½ cups (375ml) chicken stock
2 tablespoons tomato paste
3 bay leaves
4 sprigs fresh thyme
2 sprigs fresh rosemary

1 Trim green ends from onions, leaving about 4cm (1 ½ inches) of stem attached; trim roots. Heat 1 tablespoon of the oil in large frying pan; cook onions, stirring, until browned; remove from pan.
2 Add bacon, mushrooms and garlic to pan; cook, stirring, until bacon is crisp. Remove from pan.
3 Coat chicken in flour; shake off excess. Heat remaining oil in same pan; cook chicken, in batches, until browned. Drain on absorbent paper.
4 Return chicken to pan with wine, stock, paste, bay leaves, herbs, onions and bacon mixture. Bring to the boil; reduce heat, simmer, uncovered, about 35 minutes or until chicken is tender and sauce has thickened slightly.

prep + cook time 1 hour 30 minutes **serves** 4
nutritional count per serving 43.6g total fat (11.8g saturated fat); 3428kJ (820 cal); 16.3g carbohydrate; 67.8g protein; 6.4g fibre

Coq à la bière

1.4kg (2¾-pound) whole chicken
¼ cup (35g) plain (all-purpose) flour
20g (¾ ounce) butter
2 large carrots (360g)
1 tablespoon olive oil
6 shallots (150g), peeled
2 tablespoons brandy
1½ cups (375ml) pale ale
1 cup (250ml) chicken stock
1 bay leaf
2 sprigs each fresh thyme and flat-leaf parsley
20g (¾ ounce) butter, extra
200g (6½ ounces) mushrooms
½ cup (125ml) pouring cream

1 Halve chicken lengthways; cut halves crossways through the centre. Separate breasts from wings; separate thighs from legs.
2 Coat chicken pieces in flour; shake off excess. Melt butter in large saucepan; cook chicken, in batches, until browned. Remove from pan.
3 Meanwhile, cut carrots into 5cm (2-inch) lengths; cut lengths in half lengthways then cut halves thickly into strips.
4 Heat oil in same cleaned pan; cook shallots, stirring occasionally, about 5 minutes or until browned lightly. Add carrot; cook, stirring, 5 minutes. Add brandy; cook, stirring, until liquid evaporates. Add chicken, ale, stock and herbs; bring to the boil. Reduce heat; simmer, uncovered, 1¼ hours.
5 Melt extra butter in medium frying pan; cook mushrooms, stirring, until just tender. Add mushrooms and cream to chicken; cook, covered, 15 minutes.

prep + cook time 2 hours 20 minutes **serves** 4
nutritional count per serving 54.8g total fat (23.8g saturated fat); 3206kJ (767 cal); 15.1g carbohydrate; 40.5g protein; 4.9g fibre
tip Coq à la bière is a specialty of the beer-producing region of Alsace, but this recipe uses a pale ale instead of the traditional dark brew. And the result is a lighter, more delicately flavoured sauce that suits the chicken perfectly.
serving suggestion Mashed potato.

Roast bacon-wrapped quail with muscat sauce

4 quails (780g)
1 medium lemon (140g)
20g (¾ ounce) butter
4 rindless bacon slices (260g)
⅓ cup (80ml) muscat
250g (8 ounces) green beans
½ cup (125ml) chicken stock
155g (5 ounces) fresh muscatel grapes, halved

1 Preheat oven to 200°C/400°F.
2 Discard necks from quails. Wash quails under cold water; pat dry with absorbent paper.
3 Halve lemon; cut one lemon half into four wedges. Place one lemon wedge and a quarter of the butter inside each quail. Tuck legs along body, wrapping tightly with bacon rasher to hold legs in place.
4 Place quails in medium flameproof dish; drizzle with one tablespoon of the muscat and juice of remaining lemon half. Roast, uncovered, about 25 minutes or until quails are browned and cooked through. Remove quails from dish; cover to keep warm.
5 Meanwhile, boil, steam or microwave beans until tender; drain. Cover to keep warm.
6 Return dish with pan liquid to heat, add remaining muscat and stock; stir until sauce boils and reduces to about ½ cup. Add grapes; stir until heated though.
7 Serve quail on beans topped with sauce.

prep + cook time 45 minutes **serves** 4
nutritional count per serving 20.9g total fat (7.7g saturated fat); 1689kJ (404 cal); 12.4g carbohydrate; 33.8g protein; 3.6g fibre

Navarin of lamb

2 tablespoons olive oil
8 lamb noisettes (800g)
1 large brown onion (200g), sliced thickly
2 cloves garlic, crushed
2 tablespoons plain (all-purpose) flour
1 cup (250ml) water
3 cups (750ml) chicken stock
½ cup (125ml) dry red wine
400g (12½ ounces) canned diced tomatoes
¼ cup (70g) tomato paste
2 dried bay leaves
2 sprigs fresh rosemary
2 stalks celery (300g), trimmed, cut into 5cm (2-inch) lengths
150g (4½ ounces) green beans, trimmed, halved
20 baby carrots (400g), trimmed
200g (6½ ounces) mushrooms
1 cup (120g) frozen peas
½ cup coarsely chopped fresh flat-leaf parsley

1 Heat oil in large saucepan; cook lamb, in batches, until browned. Remove from pan.
2 Cook onion and garlic in same pan, stirring, until onion softens. Add flour; cook, stirring, until mixture bubbles and thickens. Gradually add the water, stock and wine; stir until mixture boils and thickens.
3 Return lamb to pan with undrained tomatoes, paste, bay leaves and rosemary; bring to the boil. Reduce heat; simmer, covered, 30 minutes.
4 Add celery, beans, carrots and mushrooms to pan; simmer, covered, about 30 minutes or until vegetables are tender. Add peas; simmer, uncovered, until peas are just tender. Season to taste.
5 Remove and discard toothpicks from lamb; serve sprinkled with parsley.

prep + cook time 2 hours **serves** 4
nutritional count per serving 32.6g total fat (12.9g saturated fat); 2913kJ (697 cal); 21.4g carbohydrate; 69.3g protein; 11g fibre
tip Lamb noisettes are lamb sirloin chops with the bone removed and the "tail" wrapped around the meaty part of the chop and secured with a toothpick.
serving suggestion Creamy celeriac or potato mash.

Garlic and sage lamb racks

3 large red onions (900g)
12 fresh sage leaves
⅓ cup (80ml) olive oil
2 tablespoons coarsely chopped fresh sage
4 cloves garlic, chopped coarsely
4 x 4 french-trimmed lamb cutlet racks (600g)

1 Preheat oven to 220°C/425°F.
2 Halve onions, slice into thin wedges; place in large baking dish with sage leaves and half the oil.
3 Combine remaining oil in small bowl with chopped sage and garlic. Press sage mixture all over lamb; place on onion in dish.
4 Roast lamb, uncovered, about 25 minutes or until lamb is browned and cooked as desired. Cover lamb racks; stand 10 minutes.

prep + cook time 35 minutes **serves** 4
nutritional count per serving 31.3g fat (8.5g saturated fat); 1676kJ (401 cal); 12.4g carbohydrate; 18.4g protein; 3.4g fibre
tip Red onions are sweet and have a less aggressive flavour than their brown and white counterparts.

Honey dijon lamb racks with potato and kumara gratin

2 tablespoons olive oil
2 teaspoons dijon mustard
¼ cup (60ml) red wine vinegar
2 cloves garlic, crushed
2 tablespoons honey
4 x 4 french-trimmed lamb cutlet racks (600g)
1 medium kumara (orange sweet potato) (400g)
2 medium potatoes (400g)
1 tablespoon plain (all-purpose) flour
1¾ cups (430ml) pouring cream
¼ cup (60ml) milk
¾ cup (75g) grated pizza cheese

1 Combine oil, mustard, vinegar, garlic and honey in large bowl; add lamb, turn to coat all over in marinade. Cover; refrigerate 3 hours or overnight.
2 Preheat oven to 200°C/400°F. Grease deep 19cm (7½-inch) square cake pan.
3 Using V-slicer, mandoline or sharp knife, cut kumara and potatoes into 2mm (⅛-inch) thick slices. Place half the kumara slices, overlapping slightly, in pan. Top with a layer using half the potato, overlapping slices slightly. Repeat layering with remaining kumara and potato.
4 Blend flour with a little of the cream in medium jug to form a smooth paste; stir in remaining cream and milk. Pour cream mixture over potato and kumara. Cover gratin with foil; bake about 45 minutes or until vegetables are tender. Uncover; sprinkle with cheese. Bake, uncovered, 15 minutes or until cheese browns. Stand gratin 5 minutes before serving.
5 Meanwhile, drain lamb; reserve marinade. Place lamb on wire rack in large shallow baking dish; roast, uncovered, for about the last 35 minutes of gratin cooking time or until cooked as desired. Cover to keep warm.
6 Bring reserved marinade to the boil in small saucepan. Reduce heat; simmer sauce, uncovered, 5 minutes.
7 Serve gratin with lamb, drizzled with sauce.

prep + cook time 1 hour 50 minutes (+ refrigeration) **serves** 4
nutritional count per serving 66.5g total fat (36.2g saturated fat); 3632kJ (869 cal); 42g carbohydrate; 27.6g protein; 3.4g fibre

Duxelles-filled leg of lamb with roasted vegetables

45g (1½ ounces) butter
155g (5 ounces) swiss brown mushrooms, chopped finely
1 clove garlic, crushed
3 shallots (75g), chopped finely
½ cup (125ml) balsamic vinegar
1.2kg (2½-pound) easy carve lamb leg
1 teaspoon sea salt
2 large parsnips (700g)
2 large carrots (360g)
1 large kumara (orange sweet potato) (500g)
2 large potatoes (600g)
2 tablespoons olive oil
½ cup (125ml) beef stock

1 Melt butter in large frying pan; cook mushrooms, garlic and shallot, stirring, until onion softens. Add half the vinegar; bring to the boil. Reduce heat; simmer duxelles, uncovered, about 5 minutes or until liquid has evaporated.
2 Fill lamb cavity with duxelles; rub lamb all over with salt.
3 Preheat oven to 180°C/350°F.
4 Halve parsnips, carrots and kumara first crossways, then lengthways; cut pieces into thick slices. Cut potatoes into wedges. Place vegetables, in single layer, in large shallow flameproof baking dish; drizzle with oil. Place lamb on wire rack over vegetables; roast, uncovered, about 1½ hours or until lamb is cooked as desired and vegetables are tender. Remove lamb and vegetables from dish, cover lamb; stand 10 minutes.
5 Meanwhile, place dish containing juices over heat; stir in stock and remaining vinegar, bring to the boil. Strain sauce into small jug.
6 Serve sliced lamb and vegetables, drizzled with sauce.

prep + cook time 2 hours 15 minutes **serves** 4
nutritional count per serving 34.3g total fat (13.9g saturated fat); 3432kJ (821 cal); 50.5g carbohydrate; 76.5g protein; 11g fibre
tip A duxelles (doo-zell) is a classic French mixture of finely chopped mushrooms and shallots cooked in butter. It is used as an ingredient in pâtés, sauces and stuffings.

Lamb bretonne

1.5kg (3 pounds) leg of lamb
1 clove garlic, sliced thinly
2 sprigs fresh rosemary
1 teaspoon sea salt flakes
½ teaspoon freshly cracked black pepper
20g (¾ ounce) butter
2 medium brown onions (300g), sliced thinly
3 cloves garlic, crushed
410g (13 ounces) canned crushed tomatoes
410g (13 ounces) canned tomato puree
2 cups (500ml) beef stock
410g (13 ounces) canned white beans, rinsed, drained

1 Preheat oven to 180°C/350°F.
2 Trim excess fat from lamb. Pierce lamb in several places with sharp knife; press sliced garlic and a little of the rosemary firmly into cuts. Rub salt and pepper over lamb.
3 Heat butter in large flameproof baking dish; cook onion and crushed garlic, stirring, until onion browns slightly. Stir in undrained tomatoes, puree, stock, beans and remaining rosemary; bring to the boil then remove from heat.
4 Place lamb, pierced-side down, on bean mixture, cover; transfer to oven. Roast 1 hour. Uncover, turn lamb carefully; cook, brushing occasionally with tomato mixture, about 1 hour or until lamb is cooked as desired.

prep + cook time 2 hours 30 minutes **serves** 4
nutritional count per serving 19.9g total fat (9.5g saturated fat); 2324kJ (556 cal); 20.2g carbohydrate; 69.8g protein; 7.7g fibre
tip Many varieties of white beans are available canned, among them cannellini, butter and haricot beans: any of these is suitable for this recipe.

Garlic and rosemary roast lamb

2kg (4 pounds) leg of lamb
3 sprigs fresh rosemary, chopped coarsely
½ teaspoon sweet paprika
1kg (2 pounds) potatoes, chopped coarsely
500g (1-pound) piece pumpkin, chopped coarsely
3 small brown onions (240g), halved
2 tablespoons olive oil
2 tablespoons plain (all-purpose) flour
1 cup (250ml) chicken stock
¼ cup (60ml) dry red wine

1 Preheat oven to 200°C/400°F.
2 Place lamb in oiled large baking dish; using sharp knife, score skin at 2cm (¾-inch) intervals, sprinkle with rosemary and paprika.
3 Roast lamb 15 minutes. Reduce oven to 180°C/350°F; roast lamb further 45 minutes or until cooked as desired.
4 Meanwhile, place potatoes, pumpkin and onions, in single layer, in large shallow baking dish; drizzle with oil. Roast for last 45 minutes of lamb cooking time.
5 Remove lamb and vegetables from oven; strain pan juices from lamb into medium jug. Cover lamb and vegetables to keep warm.
6 Return ¼ cup of the pan juices to baking dish; stir in flour, over heat about 5 minutes or until mixture bubbles and browns. Gradually add stock and wine; stir over high heat until gravy boils and thickens. Strain gravy into medium heatproof jug.
7 Slice lamb; serve with roasted vegetables and gravy.

prep + cook time 1 hour 30 minutes **serves** 6
nutritional count per serving 17.9g total fat (6.6g saturated fat); 2086kJ (499 cal); 32.3g carbohydrate; 47.7g protein; 5g fibre
tip A roast joint should be rested before serving to allow the meat to relax. The heat of the oven causes the meat fibres to tighten, so as meat rests the fibres will relax, allowing the meat juices to redistribute themselves throughout the joint. Try to carve the joint across the grain so that each slice has short fibres which feel tender to eat.

Slow-cooked lamb with white beans

1 ¼ cups (250g) dried cannellini beans
18 shallots (450g)
1 medium orange (240g), sliced thinly
3 cloves garlic, chopped coarsely
3 bay leaves
10 sprigs fresh thyme
½ teaspoon black peppercorns
3 cups (750ml) dry red wine
2 x 1kg (2-pound) lamb shoulders
1 tablespoon olive oil
3 stalks celery (450g), trimmed, cut into chunks
⅓ cup (95g) tomato paste
800g (1 ½-pound) piece pumpkin, trimmed, cut into cubes
½ cup finely chopped fresh flat-leaf parsley

1 Place beans in medium bowl, cover with water; stand overnight. Combine shallots, orange, garlic, bay leaves, thyme, peppercorns, wine and lamb in large dish. Cover; refrigerate overnight.
2 Rinse beans; drain. Place in large saucepan of boiling water; return to the boil. Reduce heat; simmer, uncovered, about 15 minutes or until beans are just tender.
3 Preheat oven to 160°C/325°F.
4 Meanwhile, drain lamb; reserve marinade. Heat oil in large flameproof dish over heat; brown one lamb shoulder at a time in dish. Remove from dish.
5 Add unstrained marinade to dish with celery and beans; bring to the boil. Add lamb to dish; transfer to oven. Roast, covered, 2 hours or until lamb starts to fall from the bones. Remove lamb from dish; cover to keep warm.
6 Stir paste and pumpkin into dish, simmer, uncovered, over heat about 15 minutes or until pumpkin is tender.
7 Serve sliced lamb with bean mixture; sprinkle with parsley and top with thinly sliced lemon rind, if you like.

prep + cook time 3 hours (+ standing & refrigeration) **serves** 6
nutritional count per serving 26.6g total fat (11g saturated fat); 2976kJ (712 cal); 29.8g carbohydrate; 61.5g protein; 12.3g fibre
tip If you don't have time to soak the beans overnight, you could use three 400g (12½ ounces) canned rinsed, drained cannellini beans, instead; add them to the dish after 1 hour of cooking time.

Char-grilled lamb cutlets with white bean puree and tapenade

800g (1½ pounds) canned white beans, rinsed, drained
1 cup (250ml) chicken stock
1 clove garlic, crushed
1 tablespoon pouring cream
2 tablespoons lemon juice
2 tablespoons olive oil
¼ cup (60g) black olive tapenade
12 french-trimmed lamb cutlets (600g)
300g (9½ ounces) baby spinach leaves

1 Bring beans and stock to the boil in medium saucepan. Reduce heat; simmer, uncovered, about 15 minutes or until liquid is absorbed. Transfer to medium bowl; mash beans with garlic, cream, juice and half the oil until smooth. Cover to keep warm.
2 Meanwhile, combine tapenade with remaining oil in small bowl.
3 Cook lamb, in batches, on heated oiled grill plate (or grill or barbecue) until cooked as desired. Cover to keep warm.
4 Boil, steam or microwave spinach until just wilted; drain.
5 Divide bean puree, spinach and lamb among serving plates; top with tapenade mixture.

prep + cook time 45 minutes **serves** 4
nutritional count per serving 25.6g total fat (9g saturated fat); 1438kJ (344 cal); 8g carbohydrate; 21.1g protein; 5g fibre
tips Many varieties of white beans are available canned, among them cannellini, butter and haricot beans: any of these is suitable for this puree. Drain beans then rinse well under cold water before using them. We find that cooking them briefly with a little liquid results in a more luscious, creamier puree.
You can buy tapenade or make your own (see recipe page 27).

Lamb backstrap with celeriac mash and watercress

1.5kg (3 pounds) celeriac (celery root), trimmed, chopped coarsely
500g (1 pound) potatoes, chopped coarsely
40g (1½ ounces) butter, softened
½ cup (125ml) pouring cream
1 clove garlic, crushed
2 teaspoons coarsely chopped fresh rosemary
¼ cup (60ml) olive oil
800g (1½ pounds) lamb backstrap
2 tablespoons balsamic vinegar
3 cups (350g) firmly packed trimmed watercress

1 Boil, steam or microwave celeriac and potato until tender; drain. Mash celeriac and potato in large bowl with butter and cream; cover to keep warm.
2 Meanwhile, combine garlic, rosemary and 1 tablespoon of the oil in large bowl; add lamb, turn to coat in mixture. Heat large oiled frying pan; cook lamb, uncovered, until browned both sides and cooked as desired. Cover lamb; stand 10 minutes then slice thickly.
3 Combine remaining oil and vinegar in small jug. Place watercress with half of the dressing in medium bowl; toss gently to combine.
4 Serve lamb with mash and watercress; drizzle with remaining dressing.

prep + cook time 45 minutes **serves** 4
nutritional count per serving 51.6g total fat (22.9g saturated fat); 3198kJ (765 cal); 26.4g carbohydrate; 49.2g protein; 12.7g fibre
tips Celeriac may not be the prettiest of vegetables, but this knobbly brown tuber is quite delicious. It has a white flesh with a subtle celery flavour and, when mashed, has the creaminess of potato. Keep peeled celeriac in acidulated water before deep-frying, boiling or eating it raw.

Cassoulet

1½ cups (300g) dried white beans
300g (9½ ounces) boned pork belly, rind removed, sliced thinly
150g (4½-ounce) piece streaky bacon, rind removed, cut into 1cm (½-inch) pieces
800g (1½-pound) piece boned lamb shoulder, cut into 2.5cm (1-inch) pieces
1 large brown onion (200g), chopped finely
1 small leek (200g), sliced thinly
2 cloves garlic, crushed
3 sprigs fresh thyme
400g (12½ ounces) canned crushed tomatoes
2 dried bay leaves
1 cup (250ml) water
1 cup (250ml) chicken stock
2 cups (140g) stale breadcrumbs
⅓ cup coarsely chopped fresh flat-leaf parsley

1 Place beans in medium bowl, cover with cold water. Stand overnight, drain; rinse under cold water, drain. Cook beans in medium saucepan of boiling water about 15 minutes or until tender; drain.
2 Preheat oven to 160°C/325°F.
3 Cook pork in large flameproof dish, pressing down with back of spoon on pork until browned; remove from dish. Cook bacon in same pan, stirring, until crisp; remove from dish. Cook lamb, in batches, in same pan, until browned. Remove from dish.
4 Cook onion, leek and garlic in same dish, stirring, until onion softens. Return meat to dish with thyme, undrained tomatoes, bay leaves, the water, stock and beans; bring to the boil. Cover; cook, in oven, 45 minutes. Remove from oven; season to taste, sprinkle with combined breadcrumbs and parsley. Cook, uncovered, in oven, about 45 minutes or until liquid is nearly absorbed and beans are tender.

prep + cook time 2 hours 50 minutes (+ standing) **serves** 6
nutritional count per serving 28.2g total fat (10.5g saturated fat); 2750kJ (658 cal); 38.5g carbohydrate; 55.8g protein; 12.4g fibre
tip This is a traditional recipe from the Languedoc region in the south west of France. There are many variations: with duck or goose fat, with or without lamb, tomato, toulouse sausages or duck confit.

Rabbit stew

2 tablespoons oil
1kg (2 pounds) rabbit pieces
3 medium brown onions (450g), sliced thickly
4 cloves garlic, crushed
410g (13 ounces) canned diced tomatoes
5 medium potatoes (1kg), chopped coarsely
2 medium carrots (240g), sliced thickly
1 cup (250ml) water
1 litre (4 cups) chicken stock
1 tablespoon balsamic vinegar
3 bay leaves
1 teaspoon dried chilli flakes
⅓ cup coarsely chopped fresh mint
1 cup (120g) frozen peas

1 Heat half the oil in large saucepan; cook rabbit, in batches, until browned. Remove from pan.
2 Heat remaining oil in same pan; cook onion and garlic, stirring, until onion softens.
3 Add undrained tomatoes, potato, carrot, the water, stock, vinegar, bay leaves, chilli and mint to pan. Return rabbit to pan; bring to the boil. Reduce heat; simmer, uncovered, 1¼ hours. Add peas; simmer, uncovered, 5 minutes.

prep + cook time 2 hours **serves** 4
nutritional count per serving 19.4g total fat (5.1g saturated fat); 2750kJ (658 cal); 44.4g carbohydrate; 70.7g protein; 10.6g fibre

Boeuf bourguignon

280g (9 ounces) baby brown onions
2 tablespoons olive oil
2kg (4 pounds) gravy beef, trimmed, chopped
30g (1 ounce) butter
2 cloves garlic, crushed
4 rindless bacon slices (260g), chopped coarsely
400g (13 ounces) button mushrooms, halved
¼ cup (35g) plain (all-purpose) flour
1¼ cups (310ml) beef stock
2½ cups (625ml) dry red wine
2 bay leaves
2 sprigs fresh thyme
½ cup coarsely chopped fresh flat-leaf parsley

1 Peel onions, leaving root end intact so onion remains whole during cooking.
2 Heat oil in large flameproof dish; cook beef, in batches, until browned. Remove from pan.
3 Add butter to dish; cook onions, garlic, bacon and mushrooms, stirring, until onions brown lightly.
4 Sprinkle flour over onion mixture; cook, stirring, until flour mixture thickens and bubbles. Gradually add stock and wine; stir over heat until mixture boils and thickens.
5 Return beef and any juices to dish, add bay leaves and thyme; bring to the boil. Reduce heat; simmer, covered, about 2 hours or until beef is tender, stirring every 30 minutes. Remove from heat; discard bay leaves. Stir in parsley.

prep + cook time 2 hours 45 minutes **serves** 6
nutritional count per serving 31.4g total fat (12.1g saturated fat); 2658kJ (636 cal); 6.6g carbohydrate; 80.3g protein; 2.8g fibre
tip This is a traditional dish from the Burgundy region (Bourgogne) known for its beef (charolais) and its wine.

Provençale beef casserole

2 tablespoons olive oil
1kg (2 pounds) gravy beef, cut into 2cm (¾-inch) pieces
2 rindless bacon slices (130g), chopped finely
1 medium leek (350g), sliced thinly
2 medium carrots (240g), chopped coarsely
1 stalk celery (150g), trimmed, chopped coarsely
2 cloves garlic, crushed
410g (13 ounces) canned crushed tomatoes
1½ cups (375ml) beef stock
1 cup (250ml) dry red wine
2 bay leaves
4 sprigs fresh thyme
6 sprigs fresh flat-leaf parsley
2 medium zucchini (240g), sliced thickly
½ cup (75g) seeded black olives

1 Heat oil in large saucepan; cook beef, in batches, until browned. Remove from pan.
2 Cook bacon, leek, carrot, celery and garlic in same pan, stirring, until leek softens.
3 Return beef to pan with undrained tomatoes, stock, wine, bay leaves, thyme and parsley; bring to the boil. Reduce heat; simmer, covered, 1 hour, stirring occasionally.
4 Add zucchini and olives; simmer, covered, about 30 minutes or until beef is tender.
5 Remove and discard bay leaves, thyme and parsley before serving.

prep + cook time 2 hours 30 minutes **serves** 4
nutritional count per serving 25.8g total fat (7.8g saturated fat); 2458kJ (588 cal); 14.1g carbohydrate; 61.4g protein; 6.4g fibre
serving suggestion Serve with crushed kipfler (fingerling) potatoes.

Pork chops with apples and calvados

4 x 280g (9½-ounce) pork loin chops
45g (1½ ounces) butter
2 medium apples (300g), peeled, cut into thin wedges
4 shallots (100g), sliced thinly
1 tablespoon plain (all-purpose) flour
½ cup (125ml) calvados
1 cup (250ml) cider vinegar
1 cup (250ml) chicken stock
⅔ cup (160ml) pouring cream

1 Cook pork in heated oiled large frying pan. Remove from pan; cover to keep warm. Drain and discard excess fat from pan.
2 Heat half the butter in pan; cook apples, stirring, until browned lightly. Remove from pan.
3 Heat remaining butter in pan; cook shallots, stirring, until soft. Add flour; cook, stirring, 1 minute. Add calvados; bring to the boil. Stir in vinegar, stock and cream; simmer, uncovered, until sauce thickens slightly. Return apples to pan; cook until heated through.
4 Serve pork topped with apples and sauce.

prep + cook time 30 minutes **serves** 4
nutritional count per serving 47.5g total fat (25g saturated fat); 2947kJ (705 cal); 18.1g carbohydrate; 35.7g protein; 1.4g fibre
tip Calvados is an apple-flavoured brandy made in Normandy.
serving suggestion Serve with a green salad.

Steak with pepper sauce

1 tablespoon olive oil
4 x 200g (6½-ounce) scotch fillet steaks
1 stalk celery (150g), trimmed, chopped finely
1 medium brown onion (150g), chopped finely
½ cup (125ml) dry white wine
1¼ cups (310ml) pouring cream
1 tablespoon mixed peppercorns, crushed
1 tablespoon coarsely chopped fresh thyme

1 Heat half the oil in large frying pan; cook steaks, in batches, until cooked as desired. Remove from pan; cover to keep warm.
2 Heat remaining oil in same pan; cook celery and onion, stirring, until vegetables soften. Add wine; stir until liquid is reduced by half. Add cream and peppercorns; bring to the boil. Reduce heat; simmer, uncovered, stirring occasionally, about 5 minutes or until sauce thickens slightly. Remove from heat; stir in thyme.
3 Serve steaks drizzled with sauce and with chips, if you like.

prep + cook time 25 minutes **serves** 4
nutritional count per serving 50.1g total fat (27.8g saturated fat); 2776kJ (664 cal); 4.8g carbohydrate; 44.4g protein; 1.4g fibre
tips Cook the vegetables in the same pan as the steak and add the wine to "deglaze" the pan. This picks up all the colour and flavour from cooking the steak, resulting in a rich sauce.
It is fine to use just one 300ml carton of cream for this recipe.
This is a classic bistro dish served throughout France.

Seared calves' liver with persillade

400g (12½-ounce) piece calves' liver, sliced thinly
50g (1½ ounces) butter
1 clove garlic, chopped finely
1 shallot (25g), chopped finely
½ cup (125ml) chicken stock
1 tablespoon lemon juice
⅓ cup finely chopped fresh flat-leaf parsley

1 Pat liver dry with absorbent paper. Melt 1 tablespoon of the butter in large frying pan; cook liver quickly, in batches, over high heat until browned both sides and cooked as desired (do not overcook). Remove from pan; cover to keep warm.
2 To make persillade, heat remaining butter in same pan; cook garlic and shallot, stirring, until shallot softens. Add stock and juice; bring to the boil, stirring. Remove from heat; stir in parsley.
3 Serve sliced liver with persillade.

prep + cook time 30 minutes **serves** 4
nutritional count per serving 18g total fat (9.1g saturated fat); 1087kJ (260 cal); 3g carbohydrate; 21.6g protein; 0.3g fibre
tip Persillade is a mixture of chopped garlic and parsley traditionally used either as a garnish or to flavour a sauce, as we have done here.
serving suggestion Serve with mashed potato and steamed asparagus.

Tournedos with tarragon butter

3 medium potatoes (600g)
4 rindless bacon slices (260g)
4 x 125g (4-ounce) beef fillet steaks

tarragon butter
60g (2 ounces) butter, softened
1 clove garlic, crushed
2 teaspoons finely chopped fresh tarragon
2 teaspoons finely grated lemon rind

1 Make tarragon butter.
2 Boil, steam or microwave whole potatoes until tender; drain. Cool slightly; slice potatoes thickly.
3 Meanwhile, wrap bacon around beef; secure with toothpicks. Cook beef in heated oiled large frying pan until cooked as desired. Cover beef; stand 5 minutes.
4 Meanwhile, add potatoes to same pan; cook until brown.
5 Place potato on serving plates; top with beef then butter slices.
tarragon butter Combine ingredients in small bowl. Place on piece of plastic wrap; shape into 6cm (2¼-inch) log, wrap tightly. Freeze until firm.

prep + cook time 30 minutes (+ freezing) **serves** 4
nutritional count per serving 25g total fat (13.2g saturated fat); 2061kJ (493 cal); 17.2g carbohydrate; 48.7g protein; 2.2g fibre

Beef sirloin with herbed butter and pommes frites

3 large potatoes (900g)
1½ tablespoons cracked black pepper
2 teaspoons salt
4 x 250g (8-ounce) beef sirloin steaks
peanut oil, for deep-frying
1 tablespoon olive oil
herbed butter
1 clove garlic
60g (2 ounces) butter, softened
2 tablespoons each finely chopped fresh basil and flat-leaf parsley

1 Cut peeled potatoes into 5mm (¼-inch) slices; cut each slice into 5mm (¼-inch) strips. Place potato in large bowl, cover with water; stand 1 hour. Drain; pat dry with absorbent paper.
2 Meanwhile, make herbed butter.
3 Combine pepper and salt on oven tray; press both sides of beef into pepper and salt mixture. Rest beef on oven tray while making frites.
4 Heat peanut oil in large saucepan or wok; cook potato, in batches, 3 minutes or until just tender, but not browned. Drain on absorbent paper.
5 Meanwhile, heat olive oil in large frying pan; cook beef until browned both sides and cooked as desired. Cover; stand 5 minutes.
6 Reheat peanut oil in pan; cook frites again, in batches, until browned lightly and crisp. Drain on absorbent paper.
7 Serve beef topped with herbed butter, accompanied with pommes frites.
herbed butter Beat ingredients in small bowl until combined. Place on piece of plastic wrap, wrap tightly, shape into rectangle; refrigerate until just firm.

prep + cook time 50 minutes (+ standing) **serves** 4
nutritional count per serving 42.8g total fat (14.7g saturated fat); 2905kJ (695 cal); 24g carbohydrate; 52.4g protein; 3.2g fibre
tips Our look at a French bistro's bifstek frites cooks a tender piece of beef to individual perfection and accompanies it with freshly made fries and a generous dab of basil-parsley butter.
The potatoes have been twice-cooked to guarantee their crispness.
We used beef sirloin with the bone in, but rib eye, fillet from the rump or eye fillet steaks are all suitable for this recipe.

Beef with herb and walnut crust

750g (1½-pound) piece beef fillet
1 tablespoon olive oil
½ cup coarsely chopped fresh flat-leaf parsley
¼ cup coarsely chopped fresh dill
1 clove garlic, crushed
2 teaspoons finely grated lemon rind
2 teaspoons lemon juice
¼ cup (30g) coarsely chopped roasted walnuts
1 tablespoon olive oil, extra

1 Preheat oven to 200°C/400°F.
2 Rub beef with oil.
3 Combine herbs and remaining ingredients in small bowl.
4 Cook beef, in flameproof baking dish, over high heat until browned.
5 Roast beef, uncovered, in oven 15 minutes. Remove, sprinkle with three-quarters of the herb mixture. Cover, return to oven; roast further 10 minutes or until beef is cooked. Stand beef 10 minutes.
6 Serve sliced beef sprinkled with remaining herb mixture.

prep + cook time 55 minutes **serves** 6
nutritional count per serving 15.5g total fat (3.7g saturated fat); 1041kJ (249 cal); 0.3g carbohydrate; 26.9g protein; 0.4g fibre

Veal medallions with sauce poivrade and potato gratin

1.2kg (2½ pounds) veal fillets
40g (1½ ounces) butter
2 shallots (50g), chopped finely
1 small carrot (70g), chopped finely
1 stalk celery (150g), trimmed, chopped finely
1 clove garlic, crushed
2 tablespoons black peppercorns, crushed
1 tablespoon plain (all-purpose) flour
2 tablespoons red wine vinegar
1 cup (250ml) dry red wine
2 cups (500ml) beef stock
2 tablespoons redcurrant jelly

potato gratin
1¾ cups (430ml) pouring cream
¾ cup (180ml) milk
2 cloves garlic, crushed
1kg (2 pounds) potatoes, cut into 2mm (⅛-inch) slices
1 medium brown onion (150g), sliced thinly
2 tablespoons finely grated parmesan cheese

1 Preheat oven to 200°C/400°F; make potato gratin.
2 Trim veal fillets; chop trimmings coarsely. Cut each fillet on the diagonal into nine slices; press with side of heavy knife or meat mallet to flatten.
3 Melt half the butter in medium saucepan; cook veal trimmings with shallot, carrot, celery, garlic and pepper, stirring, until onion softens. Add flour; cook, stirring, until mixture bubbles and thickens. Add vinegar; cook, stirring, until absorbed. Gradually add wine and stock; stir until mixture boils and thickens. Reduce heat; simmer, uncovered, until sauce reduces to about 1½ cups. Strain into small bowl; discard solids. Return sauce to same cleaned pan; whisk in jelly and remaining butter until smooth.
4 Meanwhile, cook veal in large oiled frying pan, in batches, about 45 seconds each side or until cooked as desired. Remove from pan.
5 Divide gratin among serving plates; top with veal, drizzle with sauce.
potato gratin Bring cream, milk and garlic to the boil in small saucepan. Combine potato and cream mixture in large bowl. Layer half the potato mixture in oiled deep 19cm (7½-inch) square cake pan. Layer with onion then layer with remaining potato, sprinkle with cheese. Cover with foil; bake 1 hour. Remove foil; bake further 20 minutes or until potato is tender and top lightly browned. Stand 20 minutes before serving.

prep + cook time 1 hour 50 minutes (+ standing) **serves** 6
nutritional count per serving 43.5g total fat (26.8g saturated fat); 3177kJ (760 cal); 31.8g carbohydrate; 52.1g protein; 3.5g fibre

Rare roast beef with anchovy butter

½ cup (125ml) barbecue sauce
2 cloves garlic, crushed
1 tablespoon finely chopped fresh rosemary
⅓ cup (80ml) olive oil
2kg (4-pound) boneless beef sirloin
280g (9 ounces) butter beans, trimmed
280g (9 ounces) green beans, trimmed
750g (1½ pounds) button mushrooms
2 tablespoons finely chopped fresh chives
anchovy butter
200g (6½ ounces) butter, softened
4 shallots (100g), chopped finely
1 tablespoon dijon mustard
1 tablespoon finely chopped fresh tarragon
5 drained anchovy fillets, chopped finely
1 teaspoon ground sumac

1 Preheat oven to 220°C/425°F.
2 Make anchovy butter.
3 Combine sauce, garlic, rosemary and 2 tablespoons of the oil in small bowl; rub all over beef. Place beef on oiled wire rack over baking dish; pour in enough water to half fill the dish. Roast beef 45 minutes or until cooked to your liking. Remove beef from heat, cover loosely with foil; stand 10 minutes before slicing thickly.
4 Boil, steam or microwave beans until tender; drain. Heat remaining oil in large frying pan; cook mushrooms, stirring, over medium heat until tender. Combine mushrooms and beans in large bowl; stir in chives, season to taste.
5 Divide bean and mushroom mixture among serving plates, top with beef and slices of anchovy butter.
anchovy butter Beat butter in medium bowl with electric mixer until soft; beat in remaining ingredients, season. Form into log, roll in plastic wrap; refrigerate or freeze until firm.

prep + cook time 1 hour 25 minutes (+ refrigeration) **serves** 8
nutritional count per serving 45.9g total fat (21.6g saturated fat); 2888kJ (691 cal); 11.6g carbohydrate; 57.2g protein; 4.7g fibre

Roasted beef fillet with horseradish mayonnaise

2 bunches fresh thyme
1kg (2-pound) piece beef eye fillet
2 tablespoons olive oil
1 teaspoon coarsely ground black pepper
1kg (2 pounds) potatoes, cut into chunks

horseradish mayonnaise
2 egg yolks
2 tablespoons lemon juice
¾ cup (180ml) olive oil
1 tablespoon prepared horseradish
2 tablespoons finely chopped fresh chives

1 Preheat oven to 220°C/425°F. Cover base of large shallow baking dish with thyme.
2 Trim excess fat from beef; tie with kitchen string at 3cm (1¼-inch) intervals. Brush beef all over with a little of the oil, sprinkle with pepper. Cook beef in heated large frying pan until browned; place on thyme in baking dish.
3 Toss potatoes in remaining oil then place around beef; roast, uncovered, about 25 minutes or until beef is cooked as desired.
4 Meanwhile, make horseradish mayonnaise.
5 Remove beef from dish; discard thyme. Cover beef tightly with foil. Spread potatoes in single layer in baking dish; roast, uncovered, until golden and tender.
6 Slice beef thickly; serve with mayonnaise and potatoes.
horseradish mayonnaise Blend egg yolks and juice until smooth. With motor operating, add oil in a thin, steady stream until mayonnaise thickens. Add horseradish; blend until combined. Transfer to medium bowl; stir in chives. Adjust consistency by stirring in a little hot water. Cover; refrigerate until required.

prep + cook time 1 hour **serves** 6
nutritional count per serving 45.8g total fat (9.7g saturated fat); 2792kJ (668 cal); 22.6g carbohydrate; 40.4g protein; 3.5g fibre
tips Homemade mayonnaise is not hard to make, and is worth the effort. If time is short however, buy a good-quality whole-egg mayonnaise and flavour it to taste with lemon juice, prepared horseradish and finely chopped chives. We used desiree potatoes, however, pontiac and sebago are also good – there is no need to peel them.
serving suggestion Serve with steamed baby peas.

Fillet steaks with caramelised shallots and creamy mashed potatoes

1kg (2 pounds) potatoes, chopped coarsely
50g (1½ ounces) butter, chopped
½ cup (125ml) pouring cream
16 shallots (400g)
3 green onions (scallions)
2 teaspoons olive oil
20g (¾ ounce) butter, extra
1 teaspoon light brown sugar
⅓ cup (80ml) dry red wine
2 cups (500ml) beef stock
4 x 150g (4½-ounce) beef fillet steaks

1 Boil, steam or microwave potato until tender; drain. Push potato through sieve into large bowl, add butter and cream; mash. Cover to keep warm.
2 Meanwhile, peel shallots leaving roots intact; cut green onions into 8cm (3¼-inch) lengths. Heat oil and extra butter in medium frying pan; cook shallots and green onion, stirring, until shallots are browned lightly and softened. Remove green onion from pan; reserve.
3 Add sugar to pan; cook over low heat, stirring, about 10 minutes or until shallots are caramelised.
4 Add wine and stock to pan; bring to the boil. Reduce heat; simmer, uncovered, about 10 minutes or until mixture thickens slightly. Return green onion to pan; simmer, uncovered, 2 minutes.
5 Meanwhile, cook beef on heated oiled grill plate (or grill or barbecue) until browned both sides and cooked as desired.
6 Divide mash, beef and shallot mixture among serving plates; drizzle with any remaining shallot sauce.

prep + cook time 1 hour **serves** 4
nutritional count per serving 40.1g total fat (22.4g saturated fat); 2847kJ (681 cal); 32.4g carbohydrate; 42.2g protein; 4.2g fibre
tip We used lasoda potatoes for this recipe, but you can use any floury potato, such as nicola or sebago.

Braised beef cheeks in red wine

2 tablespoons olive oil
1.6kg (3¼ pounds) beef cheeks, trimmed
1 medium brown onion (150g), chopped coarsely
1 medium carrot (120g), chopped coarsely
3 cups (750ml) dry red wine
¼ cup (60ml) red wine vinegar
800g (1½ pounds) canned whole tomatoes
¼ cup (55g) firmly packed light brown sugar
2 sprigs fresh rosemary
6 black peppercorns
2 tablespoons fresh oregano leaves
1 large fennel bulb (550g), cut into thin wedges
400g (12½ ounces) spring onions, trimmed, halved
200g (6½ ounces) swiss brown mushrooms

1 Preheat oven to 160°C/325°F.
2 Heat half the oil in large flameproof dish; cook beef, in batches, until browned. Remove from dish.
3 Heat remaining oil in same dish; cook brown onion and carrot, stirring, until onion softens. Return beef to dish with wine, vinegar, undrained tomatoes, sugar, rosemary, peppercorns, oregano and fennel; bring to the boil. Roast, covered, in the oven 2 hours.
4 Stir in spring onion and mushrooms; roast, uncovered, further 45 minutes or until beef is tender.

prep + cook time 3 hours 30 minutes **serves** 4
nutritional count per serving 41.6g total fat (14.9g saturated fat); 4188kJ (1002 cal); 30.9g carbohydrate; 90.2g protein; 9.6g fibre
serving suggestion Serve with soft polenta.

Mustard-crumbed beef fillet with rocket salad

¼ cup (70g) prepared horseradish
1 tablespoon olive oil
1kg (2-pound) piece beef eye-fillet
2 tablespoons wholegrain mustard
1 tablespoon coarsely chopped fresh flat-leaf parsley
½ cup (35g) fresh breadcrumbs
1 tablespoon butter, melted

rocket salad
100g (3 ounces) baby rocket (arugula) leaves
1 medium red onion (170g), sliced thinly
8 green onions (scallions), sliced thinly
¼ cup (40g) roasted pine nuts
⅓ cup (80ml) balsamic vinegar
⅓ cup (80ml) olive oil

1 Combine horseradish and oil in large bowl; add beef, turn to coat in mixture. Cover; refrigerate 3 hours or overnight.
2 Cook beef in heated oiled grill pan, turning, until browned. Reduce heat; cook beef, turning occasionally, about 30 minutes or until cooked. Cover; stand 10 minutes.
3 Meanwhile, make rocket salad.
4 Preheat grill (broiler).
5 Combine mustard, parsley and breadcrumbs in small bowl with half the butter. Brush beef with remaining butter; press breadcrumb mixture over beef. Grill beef until crust is browned. Stand 10 minutes; slice thickly.
6 Serve beef with rocket salad.
rocket salad Place ingredients in large bowl; toss genty to combine.

prep + cook time 1 hour 10 minutes (+ refrigeration & standing)
serves 6
nutritional count per serving 34.2g total fat (9.1g saturated fat); 2082kJ (498 cal); 8.7g carbohydrate; 38.4g protein; 1.9g fibre
tip Horseradish is sold in various forms; make sure you use the prepared white horseradish version in this recipe and not horseradish cream.

The vegetable course

Vegetable pithiviers with tomato sauce

10 large egg (plum) tomatoes (900g), quartered
2 teaspoons light brown sugar
⅓ cup (80ml) olive oil
2 tablespoons red wine vinegar
2 large red capsicums (bell peppers) (700g), halved
30g (1 ounce) butter
2 large green zucchini (300g), sliced thinly
7 flat mushrooms (560g), sliced thinly
1 clove garlic, crushed
1 tablespoon port
5 sheets puff pastry
1 egg yolk
1 tablespoon milk
50g (1½ ounces) baby spinach leaves

1 Preheat oven to 180°C/350°F. Oil oven trays.
2 Combine tomato, sugar, half the oil and half the vinegar in large bowl. Place tomatoes, skin-side down, on oven tray; roast 1 hour 40 minutes. Return tomato mixture to same bowl; crush with potato masher. Cover to keep warm; reserve tomato sauce.
3 Halve capsicums, place skin-side up, on oven tray. Roast 40 minutes or until softened. Place capsicum in plastic bag; close tightly, cool. Discard skin, membrane and seeds; slice flesh thinly.
4 Meanwhile, melt butter in large frying pan; cook zucchini, stirring, about 5 minutes or until softened. Place zucchini in small bowl; cover to keep warm. Cook mushrooms and garlic in same pan, stirring, about 5 minutes or until mushrooms soften. Add port; cook, stirring, until liquid evaporates.
5 Cut four pastry sheets into 16cm (6½-inch) squares; cut remaining sheet into quarters. Place one of the small squares on oven tray; centre 9cm (3¾-inch) cutter on pastry. Layer one-quarter of the mushroom mixture, one-quarter of the zucchini and one-quarter of the capsicum on pastry; remove cutter. Brush border with combined egg yolk and milk; top with one of the large squares, press edges together to seal.
6 Using sharp knife, cut around pithiviers, leaving 5mm (¼-inch) border; mark pastry with swirl design from centre to side, without cutting through. Brush with egg mixture. Repeat with remaining pastry, vegetables and egg mixture. Bake about 25 minutes.
7 Combine spinach, remaining oil and remaining vinegar in small bowl. Serve pithivier with tomato sauce and salad.

prep + cook time 2 hours 50 minutes **serves** 4
nutritional count per serving 74.3g total fat (10.5g saturated fat); 4824kJ (1154 cal); 90.9g carbohydrate; 23.5g protein; 12.3g fibre

Ratatouille with gremolata and goat's cheese

1 tablespoon olive oil
1 medium brown onion (150g), chopped coarsely
1 clove garlic, crushed
2 large zucchini (300g), sliced thickly
1 medium eggplant (300g), chopped coarsely
1 medium red capsicum (bell pepper) (200g), sliced thinly
1 medium green capsicum (bell pepper) (200g), sliced thinly
150g (4½ ounces) mushrooms, halved
4 medium tomatoes (600g), chopped coarsely
410g (13 ounces) canned crushed tomatoes
½ cup (125ml) water
¼ cup finely chopped fresh flat-leaf parsley
2 teaspoons finely grated lemon rind
125g (4-ounce) piece goat's cheese, crumbled

1 Heat oil in large saucepan; cook onion and garlic, stirring, until onion softens.
2 Add zucchini, eggplant, capsicums, mushrooms, fresh and undrained crushed tomatoes and the water to pan; bring to the boil. Reduce heat; simmer, uncovered, about 30 minutes or until vegetables are tender and sauce thickens slightly.
3 To make gremolata, combine parsley and rind in small bowl.
4 Divide ratatouille among serving bowls; sprinkle with gremolata then cheese.

prep + cook time 55 minutes **serves** 4
nutritional count per serving 10.6g total fat (3.9g saturated fat); 899kJ (215 cal); 14.4g carbohydrate; 11.4g protein; 8.6g fibre

Broad beans and thyme

600g (1 1/4 pounds) frozen broad (fava) beans, thawed
10g (1/2 ounce) butter
2 shallots (50g), chopped finely
150g (4 1/2 ounces) speck, chopped finely
1 tablespoon fresh thyme leaves
1 tablespoon lemon juice

1 Drop beans into medium saucepan of boiling water, return to the boil; drain. When beans are cool enough to handle, peel away grey-coloured outer shells.
2 Heat butter in large frying pan; cook shallot and speck, stirring, until speck is browned lightly. Add beans and thyme; cook, stirring, until beans are heated through. Stir in juice.

prep + cook time 40 minutes **serves** 4
nutritional count per serving 7.7g total fat (3.5g saturated fat); 589kJ (141 cal); 2g carbohydrate; 13.9g protein; 4.8g fibre
tip The flavour of these beans is musky and fresh, and they combine beautifully with mint and goat's cheese in a salad, or slip easily into a spring vegetable soup. Early in the season they are sweet; later in the season, when they become mealy, they should be pureed.

Braised baby leeks

16 baby pencil leeks (1.3kg)
30g (1 ounce) butter
⅔ cup (160ml) chicken stock
2 tablespoons dry white wine
1 teaspoon finely grated lemon rind
2 tablespoons lemon juice
¼ cup (20g) shaved parmesan cheese
¼ cup coarsely chopped fresh flat-leaf parsley

1 Carefully trim root end from leeks, leaving each leek in one piece. Trim leeks into 15cm (6-inch) lengths; halve lengthways. Rinse under cold water; drain.
2 Melt butter in large frying pan; cook leeks, 1 minute. Add stock, wine, rind and juice; bring to the boil. Reduce heat; simmer, covered, 15 minutes or until leeks are tender. Uncover; simmer about 5 minutes or until liquid has reduced by half.
3 Serve leeks drizzled with cooking liquid, sprinkled with cheese and parsley.

prep + cook time 40 minutes **serves** 4
nutritional count per serving 8.7g total fat (5.2g saturated fat); 644kJ (154 cal); 8.3g carbohydrate; 6.5g protein; 6g fibre
tip You could serve these leeks on their own as a first course, or as an impressive side to veal or fish. Be sure to supply diners with sharp knives, as even baby leeks can be hard to cut with blunt ones.

Creamed spinach

20g (¾ ounces) butter
625g (1 ¼ pounds) spinach, trimmed
½ cup (125ml) pouring cream

1 Melt butter in large frying pan; cook spinach, stirring, until wilted.
2 Add cream; bring to the boil. Reduce heat; simmer, uncovered, until liquid reduces by half.

prep + cook time 15 minutes **serves** 4
nutritional count per serving 38.7g total fat (25.4g saturated fat); 1555kJ (372 cal); 2.8g carbohydrate; 3.5g protein; 2.1g fibre

The perfect potato chip

1kg (2 pounds) bintje potatoes, peeled
peanut oil, for deep-frying

1 Cut potatoes lengthways into 1cm (½-inch) slices; cut each slice lengthways into 1cm (½-inch) wide pieces. Stand potato pieces in large bowl of cold water for 30 minutes to avoid discolouration. Drain; pat dry with absorbent paper.
2 Heat oil in deep-fryer or large saucepan; cook chips, in three batches, about 4 minutes each or until just tender but not browned. Drain on absorbent paper; stand 10 minutes.
3 Reheat oil; cook chips, in three batches, separating any that stick together by shaking deep-fryer basket or with a slotted spoon, until crisp and golden brown. Drain on absorbent paper.

prep + cook time 30 minutes **serves** 4
nutritional count per serving 14g total fat (2.5g saturated fat); 1208kJ (289 cal); 32.8g carbohydrate; 6g protein; 4g fibre
tips Russet burbank with its floury texture and low moisture content, also makes the perfect chip, but you can also use spunta.
Corn oil or vegetable oil can also be used for deep-frying.
After the first cooking, the chips can stand for several hours before the final deep-frying.

Perfect mashed potato

1kg (2 pounds) potatoes, chopped coarsely
45g (1½ ounces) butter
¾ cup (180ml) hot milk

1 Boil, steam or microwave potatoes until tender; drain.
2 Using the back of a wooden spoon; push potato through fine sieve into large bowl. Stir in butter and milk.

prep + cook time 30 minutes **serves** 4
nutritional count per serving 10.2g total fat (6.6g saturated fat); 1028kJ (246 cal); 30.1g carbohydrate; 6.7g protein; 3.4g fibre
tips Using hot milk instead of cold gives a creamier mash. Sebago, pink-eye or lasoda potatoes are all good choices.

Celeriac puree

2 cups (500ml) chicken stock
1kg (2 pounds) celeriac (celery root), trimmed, peeled, chopped coarsely
½ cup (125ml) pouring cream
1 tablespoon finely chopped fresh chives

1 Bring stock to the boil in medium saucepan; add celeriac, return to the boil. Reduce heat; simmer, covered, about 30 minutes or until celeriac is tender. Drain.
2 Blend or process celeriac in batches with cream until smooth.
3 Serve sprinkled with chives.

prep + cook time 35 minutes **serves** 4
nutritional count per serving 14.4g total fat (9.2g saturated fat); 815kJ (195 cal); 7.4g carbohydrate; 5.2g protein; 8.8g fibre
serving suggestion Serve with seafood, poultry or game birds such as quail or squab pigeon.

Sautéed potatoes (pommes sautées)

1kg (2 pounds) potatoes, unpeeled
2 tablespoons olive oil
45g (1½ ounces) butter, chopped

1 Cut potatoes into 1cm (½-inch) slices.
2 Heat oil and butter in large frying pan; cook potato, covered, over medium heat, turning occasionally, until browned. Reduce heat; cook, tossing pan to turn potato slices, about 10 minutes or until tender.

prep + cook time 25 minutes **serves** 4
nutritional count per serving 19.6g total fat (8g saturated fat); 1419kJ (339 cal); 32.8g carbohydrate; 6.1g protein; 4g fibre
tip Desiree, bintje or russet burbank potatoes are all good choices for this recipe.

Duchesse potatoes

1kg (2 pounds) nicola potatoes, peeled, chopped coarsely
3 egg yolks
100g (3 ounces) butter, melted

1 Preheat oven to 180°C/350°F. Oil two oven trays; line with baking paper.
2 Boil, steam or microwave potato until tender; drain. Mash potato in large bowl with egg yolks and butter.
3 Spoon potato mixture into large piping bag fitted with a 1cm (½-inch) fluted tube; pipe potato into 3cm (1¼-inch) rosette-shaped swirls onto oven trays.
4 Bake potatoes about 30 minutes or until browned.

prep + cook time 1 hour **makes** 40
nutritional count per rosette 2.5g total fat (1.5g saturated fat); 167kJ (40 cal); 3.3g carbohydrate; 0.8g protein; 0.4g fibre
tips You could also add ½ cup finely grated gruyère cheese to the potato with the egg yolks and butter.
The potato mixture can be piped up to 3 hours ahead; keep, covered, in the refrigerator.

Lyonnaise potatoes

900g (1¾ pounds) desiree potatoes, peeled, chopped coarsely
1 tablespoon olive oil
2 medium red onions (340g), sliced thinly
3 cloves garlic, crushed
6 rindless bacon slices (390g), chopped coarsely
¼ cup coarsely chopped fresh mint

1 Boil, steam or microwave potato until just tender; drain.
2 Meanwhile, heat half the oil in large frying pan; cook onion and garlic, stirring, until onion softens. Remove from pan.
3 Cook bacon in same pan, stirring, until crisp; drain on absorbent paper.
4 Heat remaining oil in same pan; cook potato, stirring, about 5 minutes or until browned.
5 Return onion mixture and bacon to pan; stir gently to combine with potato. Remove from heat; stir in mint.

prep + cook time 30 minutes **serves** 4
nutritional count per serving 14.2g total fat (4.1g saturated fat); 1630 kJ (390 cal); 34.7g carbohydrate; 28.1g protein; 5.1g fibre
tips Lyon is seen as one of the gastronomic capitals of the world, and it's no wonder when this French city produces luscious dishes such as this. You can also use ruby lou potatoes for this recipe.

Roasted root vegetables

2 tablespoons olive oil
12 baby carrots (240g), peeled, halved lengthways
3 small parsnips (180g), peeled, quartered lengthways
12 baby new potatoes (480g), halved
4 baby onions (100g), halved
1 clove garlic, crushed
1 tablespoon coarsely chopped fresh rosemary sprigs
1 tablespoon honey
2 teaspoons wholegrain mustard
1 tablespoon lemon juice

1 Preheat oven to 220°C/425°F.
2 Heat oil in large flameproof baking dish; cook carrot, parsnip, potato and onion, stirring, until browned. Remove dish from heat; stir in garlic, rosemary, honey and mustard.
3 Roast vegetables about 25 minutes or until vegetables are tender. Serve vegetables drizzled with juice.

prep + cook time 50 minutes **serves** 4
nutritional count per serving 4.9g total fat (0.6g saturated fat); 798kJ (191 cal); 29.3g carbohydrate; 4.5g protein; 5.3g fibre

Potatoes Anna

1.2kg (4 pounds) ruby lou potatoes, peeled
100g (3 ounces) butter, melted

1 Preheat oven to 240°C/475°F. Oil shallow 2-litre (8-cup), 26cm (10½-inch) round baking dish.
2 Using sharp knife, mandoline or V-slicer, slice potatoes into 2mm (⅛-inch) slices; pat dry with absorbent paper. Place a single layer of potato, slightly overlapping, into baking dish; brush with a little of the butter. Continue layering remaining potato and butter.
3 Cover dish with foil; bake 20 minutes. Remove foil; use metal spatula to press down on potato.
4 Reduce oven to 220°C/425°F; bake, uncovered, about 30 minutes or until top is crisp and browned. Cut into wedges to serve.

prep + cook time 1 hour 10 minutes **serves** 6
nutritional count per serving 13.9g total fat (9g saturated fat); 1066kJ (255 cal); 26.3g carbohydrate; 4.9g protein; 3.2g fibre
tips In the late 1800s, French chef Adolphe Dugléré devised this dish in honour of Anna Deslions, a courtesan who entertained clients in a private dining room within his restaurant.
You can also use coliban potatoes for this recipe.

Salads

Duck and caramelised apple salad

4 x 150g (4½-ounce) duck breasts
2 medium apples (300g), cut into thin wedges
2 tablespoons caster (superfine) sugar
150g (4½ ounces) curly endive, trimmed
½ cup (70g) coarsely chopped roasted hazelnuts
½ cup loosely packed fresh mint leaves
1 tablespoon sherry vinegar
1 tablespoon olive oil

1 Using a sharp knife, score skin on each duck breast in a 1.5cm (½-inch) diamond pattern.
2 Heat large frying pan to very hot. Place duck, skin-side down, in pan; cook about 10 minutes or until skin is golden and crisp. Turn duck over; cook 2 minutes then remove from pan. Stand duck, covered, 10 minutes.
3 Meanwhile, cook apple in same cleaned pan, stirring, 2 minutes. Add sugar; cook, stirring, about 3 minutes or until apple is browned and tender.
4 Arrange endive, nuts and mint on serving plates. Slice duck thinly then arrange on salad with apple; drizzle with combined vinegar and oil.

prep + cook time 30 minutes **serves** 4
nutritional count per serving 70.9g total fat (17.8g saturated fat); 3348kJ (801 cal); 17.6g carbohydrate; 23.2g protein; 4.3g fibre
tips The bitterness of the curly endive (the greener the leaves, the more bitter it will be) cuts through the richness of the duck and sweetness of the apple.
You can also use red wine vinegar instead of sherry vinegar.

Salad of greens, chicken livers, bacon and apple

4 rindless bacon slices (260g), sliced thinly
1 tablespoon olive oil
500g (1 pound) chicken livers, halved, trimmed
200g (6½ ounces) lamb's lettuce
250g (8 ounces) baby spinach leaves
1 medium apple (150g), halved, sliced into thin wedges
cranberry dressing
4 shallots (100g), chopped finely
2 tablespoons red wine vinegar
⅓ cup (80ml) olive oil
¼ cup (80g) whole berry cranberry sauce, warmed

1 Make cranberry dressing.
2 Cook bacon, stirring, in large frying pan until crisp; drain on absorbent paper.
3 Heat oil in same clean pan; cook liver, over high heat, about 5 minutes or until browned and cooked as desired (do not overcook or liver will be dry and tasteless). Drain on absorbent paper.
4 Place bacon and liver in large bowl with lettuce, spinach leaves, apple and dressing; toss gently to combine.
cranberry dressing Combine ingredients in small bowl.

prep + cook time 30 minutes **serves** 4
nutritional count per serving 33.7g total fat (7g saturated fat); 2149kJ (514 cal); 14g carbohydrate; 38.2g protein; 3.3g fibre
tip Lamb's lettuce, also known as mâche or corn salad, is very popular in France. It has a mild, almost nutty flavour and dark green leaves. It is usually sold in 125g (4-ounce) punnets, but the leaves probably weigh only about a quarter of that total.

Smoked trout and white bean salad

240g (7½ ounces) whole smoked trout
¼ cup (60ml) lemon juice
2 tablespoons olive oil
1 tablespoon wholegrain mustard
2 teaspoons honey
240g (13½ ounces) canned white beans, rinsed, drained
3 cups (350g) firmly packed trimmed watercress
½ cup coarsely chopped fresh flat-leaf parsley
¼ cup (45g) drained cornichons

1 Discard skin and bones from fish; flake fish into large bowl.
2 Place juice, oil, mustard and honey in screw-top jar; shake well.
3 Add remaining ingredients and dressing to bowl with fish; toss gently to combine.

prep + cook time 20 minutes **serves** 4
nutritional count per serving 11.2g total fat (1.7g saturated fat); 924kJ (221 cal); 14.1g carbohydrate; 13.4g protein; 5.7g fibre

Crunchy snow pea, prawn and avocado salad with chive vinaigrette

750g (1½ pounds) cooked medium king prawns (shrimp)
150g (4½ ounces) sugar snap peas, trimmed
3 small avocados (600g), sliced thickly
2 cups (100g) snow pea sprouts
chive vinaigrette
¼ cup (60ml) white wine vinegar
¼ cup (60ml) olive oil
¼ cup finely chopped fresh chives

1 Make chive vinaigrette.
2 Shell and devein prawns, leaving tails intact.
3 Boil, steam or microwave peas until just tender; rinse under cold water, drain.
4 Place prawns and peas in large bowl with avocado, sprouts and vinaigrette; toss gently to combine.
chive vinaigrette Combine ingredients in small bowl.

prep + cook time 25 minutes **serves** 4
nutritional count per serving 38.2g total fat (7.2g saturated fat); 1998kJ (478 cal); 8.2g carbohydrate; 24.6g protein; 3.7g fibre

Salade niçoise

3 small potatoes (360g), chopped coarsely
200g (6½ ounces) baby green beans, trimmed
2 tablespoons olive oil
1 tablespoon lemon juice
2 tablespoons white wine vinegar
4 medium tomatoes (600g), cut into wedges
4 hard-boiled eggs, quartered
425g (13½ ounces) canned tuna in springwater, drained, flaked
½ cup (80g) rinsed, drained caperberries
½ cup (60g) seeded small black olives
¼ cup firmly packed fresh flat-leaf parsley leaves

1 Boil, steam or microwave potato and beans, separately, until tender; drain. Rinse under cold water; drain.
2 Whisk oil, juice and vinegar in large bowl; add potatoes, beans and remaining ingredients, toss gently to combine.

prep + cook time 20 minutes **serves** 4
nutritional count per serving 17g total fat (3.7g saturated fat); 1530kJ (366 cal); 18.9g carbohydrate; 30.9g protein; 4.9g fibre
tip This is a specialty from Nice in the south of France.

Beef sausage and lentil salad

2 cups (400g) brown lentils
2 sprigs fresh thyme
20 baby beetroot (beets) (500g), trimmed
8 thick beef sausages (1.2kg)
2 teaspoons olive oil
1 large brown onion (200g), chopped finely
2 teaspoons each yellow mustard seeds and ground cumin
1 teaspoon ground coriander
½ cup (125ml) chicken stock
100g (3 ounces) baby spinach leaves

thyme dressing
1 teaspoon fresh thyme leaves
1 clove garlic, crushed
½ cup (125ml) red wine vinegar
¼ cup (60ml) olive oil

1 Make thyme dressing.
2 Cook lentils in large saucepan of boiling water with thyme until lentils are tender; drain, discard thyme. Combine lentils in large bowl with half the dressing.
3 Meanwhile, boil, steam or microwave unpeeled beetroot until tender; drain. When cool enough to handle, peel and halve beetroot.
4 Cook sausages in heated oiled grill pan until cooked. Stand 5 minutes, slice thickly.
5 Heat oil in small saucepan; cook onion, seeds and spices, stirring, until onion softens. Add stock; bring to the boil.
6 Add beetroot, sausages, onion mixture, spinach and remaining dressing in bowl with lentils; toss gently to combine.
thyme dressing Place ingredients in screw-top jar; shake well.

prep + cook time 1 hour 10 minutes **serves** 4
nutritional count per serving 94.5g total fat (39.2g saturated fat); 5676kJ (1358 cal); 55.8g carbohydrate; 62.8g protein; 26.4g fibre

Oven-roasted beef fillet and beetroot with horseradish crème fraîche

500g (1-pound) piece beef eye fillet, trimmed
2 tablespoons wholegrain mustard
1 tablespoon horseradish cream
2 tablespoons olive oil
1kg (2 pounds) baby beetroots (beets), trimmed
150g (4½ ounces) baby rocket (arugula) leaves
2 lebanese cucumbers (260g), sliced thinly
1 cup loosely packed fresh flat-leaf parsley leaves

gruyère croûtons
1 small french bread stick (150g)
1 tablespoon olive oil
½ cup (60g) finely grated gruyère cheese

horseradish crème fraîche
¼ cup (60g) crème fraîche
2 tablespoons horseradish cream
1 tablespoon lemon juice

1 Preheat oven to 220°C/425°F.
2 Tie beef with kitchen string at 3cm (1¼-inch) intervals. Combine mustard, horseradish and oil in small jug; brush mixture all over beef.
3 Place beef in medium oiled baking dish with beetroot; roast, uncovered, 10 minutes.
4 Reduce oven to 200°C/400°F; roast about 20 minutes or until beef and beetroot are cooked. Cover beef; stand 15 minutes then slice thinly. Peel and halve beetroots.
5 Make gruyère croûtons.
6 Make horseradish crème fraîche.
7 Combine rocket, cucumber, parsley and beetroot in large bowl.
8 Serve salad topped with croûtons and beef, drizzled with crème fraîche.
gruyère croûtons Slice bread thinly; brush slices with oil, place on oven tray. Brown, in oven, towards end of beef cooking time; sprinkle with cheese, return to oven until cheese melts.
horseradish crème fraîche Combine ingredients in small bowl.

prep + cook time 45 minutes (+ standing) **serves** 4
nutritional count per serving 35.9g total fat (12.9g saturated fat); 2834kJ (678 cal); 42.3g carbohydrate; 41.5g protein; 11.7g fibre

Pork and beetroot salad

1kg (2 pounds) baby beetroot (beets)
800g (1½ pounds) spring onions
2 tablespoons olive oil
750g (1½ pounds) pork fillets
150g (4½ ounces) mixed baby asian greens
1 cup (100g) coarsely chopped roasted walnuts

horseradish dressing
¾ cup (180g) crème fraîche
3 teaspoons dijon mustard
3 teaspoons prepared horseradish
1 tablespoon lemon juice
2 tablespoons water

1 Preheat oven to 200°C/400°F.
2 Cut stalk and root ends of beetroot to 3cm (1¼-inch) lengths; halve beetroot lengthways. Trim roots from onions; trim stems to 5cm (2 inches). Halve onions lengthways. Place beetroot and onion, in single layer, in large shallow baking dish; drizzle with half the oil. Roast, uncovered, 30 minutes or until tender.
3 Meanwhile, heat remaining oil in large frying pan; cook pork, turning, until browned and cooked as desired. Transfer pork to dish; cover to keep warm.
4 Meanwhile, make horseradish dressing.
5 Divide asian greens among serving plates; top with roasted vegetables and sliced pork. Drizzle with dressing; sprinkle with nuts.
horseradish dressing Whisk all ingredients in small jug until smooth.

prep + cook time 50 minutes **serves** 6
nutritional count per serving 33.2g total fat (10.6g saturated fat); 2249kJ (538 cal); 20.5g carbohydrate; 35.8g protein; 8.8g fibre
tip Horseradish is sold in various forms; make sure you use the prepared white horseradish version in this recipe and not horseradish cream.

Warm lentil and chorizo salad

1 ¼ cups (250g) french-style green lentils
1 small brown onion (80g), quartered
1 bay leaf
2 cured chorizo sausages (340g), sliced thinly
½ cup (125ml) red wine vinegar
⅓ cup (80ml) olive oil
3 shallots (75g), sliced thinly
2 stalks celery (300g), trimmed, sliced diagonally
1 cup coarsely chopped fresh flat-leaf parsley

1 Cook lentils, onion and bay leaf in large saucepan of boiling water, uncovered, about 15 minutes or until lentils are tender; drain. Discard onion and bay leaf.
2 Cook chorizo in large frying pan, stirring occasionally, until browned. Drain; cool 10 minutes.
3 Place vinegar and oil in screw-top jar; shake well.
4 Place lentils and chorizo in large bowl with shallot, celery, parsley and dressing; toss gently to combine.

prep + cook time 40 minutes **serves** 6
nutritional count per serving 30g total fat (8g saturated fat); 1848kJ (442 cal); 18.9g carbohydrate; 28.1g protein; 7.2g fibre
tip French-style green lentils are the Australian variety of lentils du puy. They are perfect for salads as they keep their shape after cooking.

Oak-leaf and mixed herb salad

1 green oak-leaf lettuce, leaves separated
¼ cup coarsely chopped fresh chives
½ cup each firmly packed fresh chervil leaves and flat-leaf parsley leaves
dijon vinaigrette
2 tablespoons olive oil
2 tablespoons white wine vinegar
1 tablespoon dijon mustard
2 teaspoons white sugar

1 Make dijon vinaigrette.
2 Place salad ingredients in medium bowl with dressing; toss gently to combine.
dijon vinaigrette Place ingredients in screw-top jar; shake well.

prep time 10 minutes **serves** 6
nutritional count per serving 6.2g total fat (0.9g saturated fat); 288kJ (69 cal); 2g carbohydrate; 0.7g protein; 1.1g fibre
tip The French often serve a simple salad like this between the main course and the cheese platter.

Salade composé

1 small french bread stick (150g)
2 cloves garlic, crushed
¼ cup (60ml) olive oil
6 rindless bacon slices (390g), sliced thickly
150g (4½ ounces) mesclun
6 medium egg (plum) tomatoes (450g), sliced thinly
4 hard-boiled eggs, halved lengthways
red wine vinaigrette
¼ cup (60ml) red wine vinegar
3 teaspoons dijon mustard
⅓ cup (80ml) extra virgin olive oil

1 Preheat grill (broiler).
2 Cut bread into 1cm (½-inch) slices. Brush both sides with combined garlic and oil; toast under grill.
3 Cook bacon in large frying pan until crisp; drain on absorbent paper.
4 Meanwhile, make red wine vinaigrette.
5 Layer bread and bacon in large bowl with mesclun and tomato, top with egg; drizzle with vinaigrette.
red wine vinaigrette Place ingredients in screw-top jar; shake well.

prep + cook time 35 minutes **serves** 4
nutritional count per serving 47.4g total fat (9.5g saturated fat); 2730kJ (653 cal); 23.3g carbohydrate; 31.8g protein; 3.9g fibre
tip Literally meaning "composed salad", the ingredients in this dish are layered on top of each other, rather than being tossed together, and the dressing is drizzled over the top.

Witlof, pear and roquefort salad

2 red witlof (belgian endive) (250g), trimmed, leaves separated
2 yellow witlof (belgian endive) (250g), trimmed, leaves separated
1 medium pear (230g), sliced thinly
¾ cup (90g) roasted pecans, coarsely chopped
blue cheese dressing
⅓ cup (80ml) buttermilk
100g (3 ounces) roquefort cheese, crumbled
1 tablespoon lemon juice

1 Make blue cheese dressing.
2 Place salad ingredients in large bowl; toss gently to combine.
3 Serve salad drizzled with dressing.
blue cheese dressing Whisk ingredients in small jug until smooth.

prep time 20 minutes **serves** 4
nutritional count per serving 24.9g total fat (6.5g saturated fat); 1295kJ (309 cal); 9.9g carbohydrate; 9.5g protein; 5.3g fibre
tip Witlof is a perfect addition to this bitey salad. Its bitter-yet-creamy flavour goes beautifully with the sharp taste of the blue cheese, and its crisp robust nature makes it a perfect candidate for the rich dressing. Choose another sharp blue cheese if you cannot find any roquefort.

Dill and caper potato salad

1kg (2 pounds) baby potatoes, unpeeled, halved
2 tablespoons white wine vinegar
½ cup (125ml) olive oil
½ teaspoon white sugar
1 teaspoon dijon mustard
⅓ cup (65g) drained baby capers, rinsed
⅔ cup (140g) drained pickled cocktail onions, halved
1 cup (200g) drained cornichons, halved lengthways
2 tablespoons coarsely chopped fresh dill

1 Boil, steam or microwave potato until just tender; drain.
2 Meanwhile, place vinegar, oil, sugar and mustard in screw-top jar; shake well.
3 Combine potato and half the dressing in large bowl; cool 10 minutes.
4 Add capers, onion, cornichon, dill and remaining dressing to salad; toss gently to combine.

prep + cook time 30 minutes **serves** 4
nutritional count per serving 28.8g total fat (4g saturated fat); 1885kJ (451 cal); 40g carbohydrate; 6.4g protein; 5.1g fibre
tip You can buy pickled cocktail onions and cornichons from most supermarkets. You can also use pink fir apple or ruby lou potatoes for this recipe.

Pear and roquefort salad

1 small french bread stick (150g), sliced thinly
100g (3 ounces) roquefort cheese, softened
2 small pears (360g), sliced thinly
1 cup (110g) coarsely chopped roasted walnuts
1 butter lettuce, leaves separated
100g (3 ounces) baby spinach leaves

buttermilk dressing
¼ cup (60ml) buttermilk
1 tablespoon lemon juice
1 tablespoon olive oil
½ teaspoon caster (superfine) sugar
1 clove garlic, crushed

1 Preheat oven to 200°C/400°F.
2 Place bread on oven tray; toast, in oven, until browned both sides.
3 Meanwhile, make buttermilk dressing.
4 Spread toast with cheese.
5 Place remaining ingredients in large serving bowl with dressing; toss gently to combine. Serve salad with cheese toast.

buttermilk dressing Whisk ingredients in medium bowl.

prep + cook time 20 minutes **serves** 4
nutritional count per serving 33.7g total fat (7.4g saturated fat); 2082kJ (498 cal); 31.2g carbohydrate; 14.6g protein; 7.7g fibre

Grilled goat's cheese salad

1 small french bread stick (150g), sliced thinly
2 tablespoons olive oil
½ cup (50g) roasted walnuts, coarsely chopped
⅓ cup coarsely chopped fresh flat-leaf parsley
1 clove garlic, chopped finely
2 tablespoons walnut oil
1 tablespoon white wine vinegar
300g (9½ ounces) log goat's cheese (with rind), cut into 4 slices
80g (2½ ounces) mesclun

1 Brush bread with olive oil; cook on heated oiled grill plate (or grill or barbecue) until browned both sides.
2 Meanwhile, combine nuts, parsley, garlic, walnut oil and vinegar in small bowl.
3 Preheat grill (broiler). Place cheese slices on oven tray; cook, under grill, until browned.
4 Divide mesclun among serving plates; top with cheese and walnut mixture, serve with bread.

prep + cook time 20 minutes **serves** 4
nutritional count per serving 34.4g total fat (10.2g saturated fat); 1952kJ (467 cal); 21.8g carbohydrate; 16.6g protein; 3.5g fibre

Shaved fennel and apple salad with brie and pecans

2 baby fennel (260g)
2 medium green apples (300g)
1 cup (120g) roasted pecans
1 red coral lettuce, trimmed, chopped coarsely
150g (4½ ounces) brie cheese, sliced thinly
mustard vinaigrette
⅓ cup (80ml) olive oil
¼ cup (60ml) lemon juice
1 tablespoon wholegrain mustard

1 Make mustard vinaigrette.
2 Trim and halve fennel; reserve 2 tablespoons coarsely chopped frond-tips. Halve and core unpeeled apples. Using a very sharp knife, mandoline or V-slicer, slice fennel and apple thinly.
3 Combine fennel and apple in large bowl with reserved frond tips, nuts and dressing; serve on top of lettuce with cheese.
mustard vinaigrette Place ingredients in screw-top jar; shake well.

prep time 20 minutes **serves** 6
nutritional count per serving 33.3g total fat (6.8g saturated fat); 1496kJ (358 cal); 6.6g carbohydrate; 7.4g protein; 3.5g fibre

Goat's cheese, fig and prosciutto salad

6 slices prosciutto (90g)
120g (4 ounces) baby rocket (arugula) leaves, trimmed
4 large fresh figs (320g), quartered
150g (4½ ounces) soft goat's cheese, crumbled

honey cider dressing

¼ cup (60ml) cider vinegar
2 tablespoons olive oil
1 tablespoon wholegrain mustard
1 tablespoon honey

1 Preheat grill (broiler).
2 Make honey cider dressing.
3 Cook prosciutto under grill until crisp; drain, chop coarsely.
4 Serve rocket topped with figs, cheese and prosciutto; drizzle with dressing.

honey cider dressing Place ingredients in screw-top jar; shake well.

prep + cook time 15 minutes **serves** 4
nutritional count per serving 16.9g total fat (5.7g saturated fat); 1062kJ (254 cal); 13.7g carbohydrate; 11.1g protein; 2.6g fibre

Celeriac remoulade

⅓ cup (100g) mayonnaise
1 clove garlic, crushed
⅓ cup (80g) sour cream
2 tablespoons lemon juice
2 teaspoons dijon mustard
650g (1¼ pounds) celeriac (celery root), trimmed, grated coarsely
½ cup coarsely chopped fresh flat-leaf parsley

1 Combine mayonnaise, garlic, sour cream, juice and mustard in medium bowl.
2 Stir in celeriac and parsley.

prep time 10 minutes **serves** 4
nutritional count per serving 16.3g total fat (6.2g saturated fat); 920kJ (220 cal); 12.3g carbohydrate; 3.1g protein; 6.4g fibre

Green bean and tomato salad with mustard hazelnut dressing

200g (6½ ounces) green beans, trimmed
250g (8 ounces) cherry tomatoes, halved
mustard hazelnut dressing
½ cup (70g) roasted hazelnuts, skinned, chopped coarsely
2 tablespoons hazelnut oil
2 tablespoons cider vinegar
1 teaspoon wholegrain mustard

1 Make mustard hazelnut dressing.
2 Boil, steam or microwave beans until tender; drain. Rinse under cold water; drain.
3 Place beans, tomato and dressing in medium bowl; toss gently to combine.
mustard hazelnut dressing Place ingredients in screw-top jar; shake well.

prep + cook time 20 minutes **serves** 4
nutritional count per serving 20.2g total fat (1.8g saturated fat); 920kJ (220 cal); 3.6g carbohydrate; 4.2g protein; 4.3g fibre

Desserts

Crème caramel

¾ cup (165g) caster (superfine) sugar
½ cup (125ml) water
6 eggs
1 teaspoon vanilla extract
½ cup (75g) caster (superfine) sugar, extra
1¼ cups (310ml) thickened (heavy) cream
1¾ cups (430ml) milk

1 Preheat oven to 160°C/325°F.
2 Stir sugar and the water in medium heavy-based frying pan over heat, without boiling, until sugar dissolves. Bring to the boil; boil, uncovered, without stirring, until mixture is a deep caramel colour. Remove from heat; allow bubbles to subside. Pour toffee into deep 20cm (8-inch) round cake pan.
3 Whisk eggs, extract and extra sugar in large bowl.
4 Bring cream and milk to the boil in medium saucepan. Whisking constantly, pour hot milk mixture into egg mixture. Strain mixture into cake pan.
5 Place pan in baking dish; add enough boiling water to come half way up side of pan. Bake about 40 minutes or until set.
6 Remove crème caramel from baking dish. Cover; refrigerate overnight.
7 Gently ease crème caramel from side of pan; invert onto deep-sided serving plate.

prep + cook time 1 hour (+ refrigeration) **serves** 8
nutritional count per serving 22.3g total fat (13.3g saturated fat); 1526kJ (365 cal); 33.8g carbohydrate; 7.5g protein; 0g fibre
tip It is fine to use just one 300ml carton of cream for this recipe.

Crème brûlée

1 vanilla bean
3 cups (750ml) thickened (heavy) cream
6 egg yolks
¼ cup (55g) caster (superfine) sugar
¼ cup (40g) pure icing (confectioners') sugar

1 Preheat oven to 180°C/350°F. Grease six ½-cup (125ml) ovenproof dishes.
2 Split vanilla bean in half lengthways; scrape seeds into medium heatproof bowl. Place pod in small saucepan with cream; heat without boiling.
3 Add egg yolks and caster sugar to seeds in bowl; gradually whisk in hot cream mixture. Place bowl over medium saucepan of simmering water; stir over heat about 10 minutes or until custard mixture thickens slightly and coats the back of a spoon. Discard pod.
4 Place small dishes in large baking dish; spoon custard into dishes. Add enough boiling water to baking dish to come halfway up sides of small dishes.
5 Bake custards, uncovered, about 20 minutes or until set. Remove custards from dish; cool. Cover; refrigerate overnight.
6 Preheat grill (broiler).
7 Place custards in shallow flameproof dish filled with ice cubes; sprinkle custards evenly with sifted icing sugar. Using finger, spread sugar over the surface of each custard, pressing in gently; place under grill until the tops caramelise.

prep + cook time 55 minutes (+ refrigeration) **serves** 6
nutritional count per serving 52.1g total fat (32.3g saturated fat); 2358kJ (564 cal); 19.8g carbohydrate; 5.8g protein; 8g fibre
tips Make sure you place the crème brûlées as close as possible to the hot grill. Surrounding the custards with ice keeps them cool as you heat the top. Of course, you could use a blowtorch if you have one. The adjustable flame melts the sugar quickly so the filling remains cool. Professional cooks' blowtorches are available from specialty kitchen shops.

Plum clafoutis

10 small plums (750g), halved, seeded
¼ cup (60ml) water
1 cinnamon stick, halved
¼ cup (55g) light brown sugar
⅔ cup (160ml) milk
⅔ cup (160ml) pouring cream
1 teaspoon vanilla extract
4 eggs
½ cup (110g) caster (superfine) sugar
¼ cup (35g) plain (all-purpose) flour

1 Preheat oven to 200°C/400°F. Grease shallow 2.5-litre (10-cup) ovenproof dish.
2 Place plums in medium baking dish with the water and cinnamon; sprinkle with brown sugar. Cook, in oven, about 15 minutes or until plums soften.
3 Remove cinnamon from dish and place in medium saucepan with milk, cream and extract; bring to the boil. Cool; remove cinnamon stick.
4 Whisk eggs and caster sugar in medium bowl until light and frothy; whisk in flour then whisk mixture into cream mixture.
5 Place drained plums in shallow ovenproof dish; pour cream mixture over plums.
6 Bake clafoutis about 30 minutes or until golden. Serve dusted with icing sugar, if you like.

prep + cook time 1 hour (+ cooling) **serves** 8
nutritional count per serving 22.3g total fat (13.3g saturated fat); 1526kJ (365 cal); 33.8g carbohydrate; 7.5g protein; 0g fibre
tip Traditional clafoutis from the Limousin region in central France is made with unpitted cherries. But this batter works with many fruit such as stone fruit, apples or berries.

Tarte tatin

6 large apples (1.2kg)
100g (3 ounces) unsalted butter, chopped
1 cup (220g) firmly packed brown sugar
2 tablespoons lemon juice
pastry
1 cup (150g) plain (all-purpose) flour
2 tablespoons caster (superfine) sugar
80g (2¾ ounces) cold unsalted butter, chopped
2 tablespoons sour cream

1 Peel, core and quarter apples. Melt butter in large heavy-based frying pan; add apple, sprinkle evenly with sugar and juice. Cook, uncovered, over low heat, 1 hour, turning apple as it caramelises.
2 Place apple, rounded-side down, in 24cm (9½-inch) pie dish; drizzle with 1 tablespoon of the caramel in pan. Reserve remaining caramel. Pack apples tightly to avoid any gaps. Cover; refrigerate until required.
3 Make pastry.
4 Preheat oven to 200°C/400°F.
5 Roll dough between sheets of baking paper until large enough to cover apple. Peel away one sheet of baking paper; invert pastry over apple. Remove remaining paper; tuck pastry around apple.
6 Bake tarte tartin about 30 minutes or until browned. Carefully turn onto serving plate.
7 Reheat reserved caramel over low heat; drizzle over apples.
pastry Process flour, sugar, butter and sour cream until ingredients just come together. Knead dough on floured surface until smooth. Cover; refrigerate 30 minutes.

prep + cook time 2 hours 30 minutes (+ refrigeration) **serves** 8
nutritional count per serving 21.1g total fat (13.7g saturated fat); 1860kJ (445 cal); 59.5g carbohydrate; 2.7g protein; 2.9g fibre

Caramelised apple tarts

50g (1½ ounces) butter
¼ cup (55g) firmly packed light brown sugar
½ teaspoon ground cinnamon
4 small apples (520g), peeled, cored, sliced thinly
½ cup (50g) roasted pecans
¼ cup (75g) apple sauce
2 teaspoons lemon juice
2 sheets butter puff pastry
1 egg

1 Stir butter, sugar and cinnamon in large frying pan over low heat until sugar dissolves. Add apple; cook, stirring occasionally, over low heat, until apple softens. Drain apple mixture over medium bowl; reserve caramel syrup.
2 Meanwhile, blend or process nuts, apple sauce and juice until smooth.
3 Preheat oven to 200°C/400°F. Grease oven tray; line with baking paper.
4 Cut eight 11cm (4½-inch) rounds from pastry sheets. Place four rounds on oven tray; brush with egg. Using 9cm (3¾-inch) cutter, remove centres from remaining rounds; position pastry rings on the 11cm (4½-inch) rounds. Spread nut mixture in centre of rounds; top with apple.
5 Bake tarts about 15 minutes. Serve warm with reheated reserved caramel syrup.

prep + cook time 30 minutes **serves** 4
nutritional count per serving 39.8g total fat (18g saturated fat); 2642kJ (632 cal); 60.5g carbohydrate; 8.3g protein; 4.3g fibre
tip Apple sauce is available from supermarkets. However, you can stew and puree your own apples if you like, or, buy canned pureed apple usually sold for babies. Any of the above will be fine for this recipe.

Apple cinnamon tarts

1 large golden delicious apple (200g)
1 sheet sweet puff pastry
20g (¾ ounce) butter, melted
1 teaspoon cinnamon sugar
¼ cup (80g) apricot jam (conserve), warmed

1 Preheat oven to 220°C/425°F. Grease oven tray.
2 Peel, core and halve apple; slice thinly.
3 Cut pastry sheet in half to form two rectangles; place on tray. Overlap apple slices down centre of pastry halves. Brush apple with butter; sprinkle with cinnamon sugar.
4 Bake tarts about 15 minutes or until pastry is browned. Brush hot tarts with jam.

prep + cook time 30 minutes **serves** 4
nutritional count per serving 13.6g total fat (3.4g saturated fat); 1120kJ (268 cal); 34g carbohydrate; 2.5g protein; 1.5g fibre
tip Cinnamon sugar is available in the spices section in the supermarket. To make your own, combine 1 teaspoon caster (superfine) sugar with a pinch of cinnamon.

Crêpes suzette

¾ cup (110g) plain (all-purpose) flour
3 eggs
2 tablespoons vegetable oil
¾ cup (180ml) milk
orange sauce
125g (4 ounces) unsalted butter
½ cup (110g) caster (superfine) sugar
1½ cups (375ml) orange juice
2 tablespoons lemon juice
⅓ cup (80ml) orange-flavoured liqueur

1 Sift flour into medium bowl, make well in centre; add eggs and oil then gradually whisk in milk until smooth. Pour batter into large jug. Cover; stand 1 hour.
2 Heat greased heavy-based crêpe pan or small frying pan; pour ¼ cup of batter into pan, tilting pan to coat base. Cook, over low heat, until browned, loosening edge of crêpe with spatula. Turn crêpe; brown other side. Remove crêpe from pan; cover to keep warm. Repeat with remaining batter to make a total of eight crêpes, greasing pan each time.
3 Make orange sauce.
4 Fold crêpes in half then in half again, place in sauce; warm over low heat. Remove crêpes to serving plates; pour hot sauce over crêpes. Serve with orange segments, if you like.
orange sauce Melt butter in large frying pan, add sugar; cook, stirring, until mixture begins to brown. Add strained juices; bring to the boil. Reduce heat; simmer, uncovered, about 3 minutes or until a golden colour. Remove from heat; add liqueur, ignite.

prep + cook time 1 hour 40 minutes (+ standing) **serves** 4
nutritional count per serving 41g total fat (20.5g saturated fat); 3039kJ (727 cal); 66.9g carbohydrate; 10.3g protein; 1.3g fibre
tips Be very careful when igniting the sauce – use extra long matches, available from most supermarkets or camping stores. Igniting the sauce burns off the alcohol, leaving a more intense flavour. If you prefer, the sauce can be served as is, without first igniting it.
Make sure overhead exhaust fans are turned off before igniting the orange sauce.

Lemon meringue pie

½ cup (75g) pure cornflour (cornstarch)
1 cup (220g) caster (superfine) sugar
½ cup (125ml) lemon juice
1¼ cups (310ml) water
2 teaspoons finely grated lemon rind
60g (2 ounces) unsalted butter, chopped
3 eggs, separated
½ cup (110g) caster (superfine) sugar, extra
pastry
1½ cups (225g) plain (all-purpose) flour
1 tablespoon icing (confectioners') sugar
140g (4½ ounces) cold butter, chopped coarsely
1 egg yolk
2 tablespoons cold water

1 Make pastry.
2 Grease 24cm (9½-inch) round loose-based fluted flan tin. Roll pastry between sheets of baking paper until large enough to line tin. Ease pastry into tin, press into base and side; trim edge. Cover; refrigerate 30 minutes.
3 Preheat oven to 240°C/475°F.
4 Place tin on oven tray. Line pastry case with baking paper; fill with dried beans or rice. Bake 15 minutes; remove paper and beans. Bake about 10 minutes; cool pie shell, turn oven off.
5 Meanwhile, combine cornflour and sugar in medium saucepan; gradually stir in juice and the water until smooth. Cook, stirring, over high heat, until mixture boils and thickens. Reduce heat; simmer, stirring, 1 minute. Remove from heat; stir in rind, butter and egg yolks. Cool 10 minutes.
6 Spread filling into pie shell. Cover; refrigerate 2 hours.
7 Preheat oven to 240°C/425°F.
8 Beat egg whites in small bowl with electric mixer until soft peaks form; gradually add extra sugar, beating until sugar dissolves.
9 Roughen surface of filling with fork before spreading with meringue mixture. Bake about 2 minutes or until browned.
pastry Process flour, icing sugar and butter until crumbly. Add egg yolk and the water; process until ingredients come together. Knead dough on floured surface until smooth. Cover; refrigerate 30 minutes.
prep + cook time 1 hour 10 minutes (+ refrigeration) **serves** 10
nutritional count per serving 18.9g total fat (11.6g saturated fat); 1772kJ (424 cal); 57.7g carbohydrate; 5g protein; 0.9g fibre

Genoise sponge

4 eggs
½ cup (110g) caster (superfine) sugar
⅔ cup (100g) plain (all-purpose) flour
60g (2 ounces) butter, melted
1¼ cups (310ml) thickened (heavy) cream
1 tablespoon icing (confectioners') sugar
¼ cup (80g) strawberry jam (conserve), warmed
500g (1 pound) strawberries, sliced thinly
1 tablespoon icing (confectioners') sugar, extra

1 Preheat oven to 180°C/350°F. Grease deep 20cm (8-inch) round cake pan; line base with baking paper.
2 Place eggs and sugar in large heatproof bowl over large saucepan of simmering water (do not allow water to touch base of bowl). Beat with electric mixer about 10 minutes or until thick and creamy. Remove bowl from pan; beat mixture until it returns to room temperature.
3 Triple sift the flour. Sift half of the flour over egg mixture, carefully fold in flour; fold in remaining sifted flour. Quickly fold in cooled butter. Pour mixture into pan.
4 Bake sponge about 20 minutes. Turn sponge, top-side up, onto baking-paper-covered wire rack to cool.
5 Beat cream and sifted icing sugar in small bowl with electric mixer until soft peaks form.
6 Split sponge in half; place one half, cut-side up, on serving plate. Spread with jam and cream; top with strawberries, then remaining sponge half. Dust with extra sifted icing sugar.

prep + cook time 1 hour 10 minutes (+ refrigeration & cooling)
serves 8
nutritional count per serving 23.4g total fat (14.4g saturated fat); 1350kJ (323 cal); 35.3g carbohydrate; 6.6g protein; 2g fibre
tips It is fine to use just one 300ml carton of cream for this recipe. This cake differs from other sponge cakes in that whole eggs are beaten over heat, then cooled. The melted butter adds to the sponge's keeping qualities.

Almond pear flan

1 1/4 cups (185g) plain (all-purpose) flour
1/4 cup (55g) caster (superfine) sugar
90g (3 ounces) butter
2 egg yolks
3 firm ripe medium pears (690g), peeled, cored, quartered
2 tablespoons apricot jam (conserve), warmed, strained
almond filling
125g (4 ounces) butter, softened
1/3 cup (75g) caster (superfine) sugar
2 eggs
1 cup (120g) ground almonds
1 tablespoon plain (all-purpose) flour

1 Process flour, sugar and butter until crumbly. Add egg yolks, process until ingredients just come together. Knead dough on floured surface until smooth. Cover; refrigerate 30 minutes.
2 Meanwhile, make almond filling.
3 Preheat oven to 180°C/350°F. Grease 24cm (9½-inch) round loose-based fluted flan tin.
4 Roll dough between sheets of baking paper until large enough to line tin. Lift pastry into tin, ease into base and side; trim edge.
5 Spread filling into pastry case; place pears over filling.
6 Bake flan about 45 minutes. Brush flan with jam.
almond filling Beat butter and sugar in small bowl with electric mixer until combined. Beat in eggs, one at a time. Stir in ground almonds and flour.

prep + cook time 1 hour 15 minutes (+ refrigeration) **serves** 10
nutritional count per serving 26.7g total fat (12.7g saturated fat); 1751kJ (419 cal); 38.4g carbohydrate; 6.9g protein; 2.8g fibre
tip Egg yolks are the only "liquid" in this pastry, so be quick about mixing them into the flour/butter mixture. Pulse the ingredients until they barely come together.

Prune and custard tart

1 ½ cups (250g) seeded prunes
2 tablespoons brandy
1 ¼ cups (310ml) pouring cream
3 eggs
⅔ cup (150g) caster (superfine) sugar
1 teaspoon vanilla extract
pastry
1 ¼ cups (175g) plain (all-purpose) flour
⅓ cup (55g) icing (confectioners') sugar
¼ cup (30g) ground almonds
125g (4 ounces) cold butter, chopped coarsely
1 egg yolk
1 tablespoon iced water, approximately

1 Make pastry.
2 Grease 26cm (10½-inch) round loose-based fluted flan tin. Roll pastry between sheets of baking paper until large enough to line tin. Lift pastry into tin, ease into base and side; trim edge, prick base all over with fork. Refrigerate 20 minutes.
3 Preheat oven to 200°C/400°F. Place tin on oven tray. Line pastry with baking paper; fill with dried beans or rice. Bake 10 minutes. Remove paper and beans; bake about 5 minutes. Cool.
4 Reduce oven to 150°C/300°F.
5 Blend or process prunes and brandy until combined; spread mixture into pastry case.
6 Bring cream to the boil in small saucepan; remove from heat. Whisk eggs, sugar and extract in small bowl, whisk in hot cream. Pour custard into pastry case; bake about 20 minutes or until custard sets. Stand 10 minutes before serving.
pastry Process flour, sugar, ground almonds and butter until crumbly. Add egg yolk and enough of the water to process until ingredients just come together. Enclose in plastic wrap; refrigerate 30 minutes.

prep + cook time 55 minutes (+ refrigeration, cooling & standing)
serves 12
nutritional count per serving 23.1g total fat (13.7g saturated fat); 1404kJ (336 cal); 37.7g carbohydrate; 5g protein; 2.4g fibre
tip It is fine to use just one 300ml carton of cream for this recipe.

Rhubarb and almond jalousie

2 cups (250g) chopped rhubarb
1/3 cup (75g) caster (superfine) sugar
2 sheets puff pastry
1 tablespoon apricot jam (conserve)
1 egg white
1 tablespoon caster (superfine) sugar, extra
frangipane filling
30g (1 ounce) butter, softened
1/4 teaspoon vanilla extract
1/4 cup (55g) caster (superfine) sugar
1 egg
1 tablespoon plain (all-purpose) flour
2/3 cup (80g) ground almonds

1 Cook rhubarb and sugar in medium saucepan over low heat, stirring, until sugar dissolves and rhubarb softens.
2 Preheat oven to 200°C/400°F. Grease oven tray.
3 Make frangipane filling.
4 Cut one pastry sheet into 14cm x 24cm (5½-inch x 9½-inch) rectangle; place on oven tray, spread with jam. Cut remaining pastry sheet into 16cm x 24cm (6-inch x 9½-inch) rectangle; leaving 2cm (¾-inch) border around all sides, make about eight evenly spaced cuts across the width of the pastry.
5 Spread frangipane filling over jam, leaving 2cm (¾-inch) border around edges; top evenly with rhubarb mixture. Brush around border with a little egg white. Place the pastry sheet with cuts over filling; press edges of pastry together to seal. Brush with egg white; sprinkle with extra sugar.
6 Bake jalousie about 35 minutes or until browned lightly and cooked through. Serve warm or cool.
frangipane filling Beat butter, extract and sugar in small bowl with electric mixer until creamy. Beat in egg; stir in flour and ground almonds.

prep + cook time 1 hour **serves** 8
nutritional count per serving 18.9g total fat (3.3g saturated fat); 1446kJ (346 cal); 37.6g carbohydrate; 6.4g protein; 2.2g fibre

Raspberry nougat frozen parfait

2 cups (400g) ricotta cheese
¾ cup (165g) caster (superfine) sugar
¼ cup (40g) whole almonds, roasted, chopped coarsely
150g (4½ ounces) nougat, chopped coarsely
1¼ cups (310ml) thickened (heavy) cream
1 cup (135g) frozen raspberries

1 Line base and sides of 14cm x 21cm (5½-inch x 8½-inch) loaf pan with foil or baking paper, extending foil 5cm (2 inches) over two long sides.
2 Blend or process cheese and sugar until smooth; transfer to large bowl. Stir in nuts and nougat.
3 Beat cream in small bowl with electric mixer until soft peaks form. Fold cream into cheese mixture; fold in raspberries.
4 Spoon mixture into pan, cover with foil; freeze until firm.
5 Slice parfait, then refrigerate about 30 minutes before serving, to soften slightly. Serve with fresh raspberries, if you like.

prep + cook time 25 minutes (+ freezing & refrigeration) **serves** 8
nutritional count per serving 24.5g total fat (13.5g saturated fat); 1329kJ (318 cal); 37.4g carbohydrate; 8.1g protein; 1.4g fibre
tips It is fine to use just one 300ml carton of cream for this recipe. The parfait can be made a week ahead up to step 3; slice with a knife that has been dipped in hot water, before allowing to soften in the refrigerator (step 5).
serving suggestion Raspberry compote: cook 2½ cups (330g) frozen raspberries and ¼ cup (55g) caster (superfine) sugar in medium saucepan, stirring, over low heat, until berries are very soft. Push mixture through coarse sieve into medium bowl; discard seeds. Just before serving, stir 500g (1 pound) fresh raspberries into berry sauce.

Berry frangipane tart

1 sheet sweet puff pastry
300g (9½ ounces) frozen mixed berries
frangipane
80g (2½ ounces) butter, softened
½ teaspoon vanilla extract
⅓ cup (75g) caster (superfine) sugar
2 egg yolks
1 tablespoon plain (all-purpose) flour
1 cup (120g) ground almonds

1 Preheat oven to 220°C/425°F. Grease 20cm x 30cm (8-inch x 12-inch) lamington pan.
2 Roll pastry until large enough to cover base and sides of pan. Line pan with pastry, press into sides. Prick pastry all over with fork; freeze 5 minutes.
3 Place another lamington pan on top of pastry; bake 5 minutes. Remove top pan; bake about 5 minutes or until pastry is browned. Cool 5 minutes. Reduce oven to 180°C/350°F.
4 Meanwhile, make frangipane.
5 Spread frangipane over pastry base. Sprinkle with berries, press into frangipane.
6 Bake tart about 30 minutes or until browned. Serve dusted with icing sugar, if you like.
frangipane Beat butter, extract, sugar and egg yolks in small bowl with electric mixer until light and fluffy. Stir in flour and ground almonds.

prep + cook time 50 minutes **serves** 6
nutritional count per serving 30.2g total fat (11.9g saturated fat); 1722kJ (412 cal); 26.4g carbohydrate; 7.7g protein; 3.3g fibre

Sweet almond cherry tarts

1 ½ cups (225g) plain (all-purpose) flour
150g (4½ ounces) butter, chopped coarsely
⅓ cup (55g) icing (confectioners') sugar
2 tablespoons iced water, approximately
2⅓ cups (350g) cherries, seeded
2 tablespoons white sugar
almond filling
60g (2 ounces) butter, softened
⅓ cup (75g) firmly packed light brown sugar
1 egg
1 tablespoon plain (all-purpose) flour
1 cup (120g) ground almonds

1 Process flour, butter and icing sugar until crumbly. Add enough of the water to process until ingredients just come together. Knead on floured surface until smooth. Enclose in plastic wrap; refrigerate 30 minutes.
2 Preheat oven to 200°C/400°F. Grease four oven trays; line with baking paper.
3 Make almond filling.
4 Divide pastry into eight pieces. Roll each piece into 15cm (6-inch) round on floured surface; place two rounds on each tray. Divide almond filling among rounds, leaving a 4cm (1½-inch) border. Top with cherries; fold over border. Sprinkle with white sugar.
5 Bake tarts about 20 minutes or until pastry is browned.
almond filling Beat butter, sugar and egg in small bowl with electric mixer until smooth. Stir in flour and ground almonds.

prep + cook time 45 minutes (+ refrigeration) **makes** 8
nutritional count per tart 29.5g total fat (14.9g saturated fat); 1990kJ (476 cal); 44.6g carbohydrate; 7g protein; 2.7g fibre
serving suggestion Serve with thick cream or vanilla ice-cream.

Roasted nectarine tart

1⅔ cups (250g) plain (all-purpose) flour
⅔ cup (110g) icing (confectioners') sugar
125g (4 ounces) cold butter
1 egg yolk
1½ tablespoons cold water
8 nectarines (1.3kg), halved, stones removed
¼ cup (60ml) orange juice
½ cup (110g) firmly packed light brown sugar

crème pâtissière
1¼ cups (310ml) thickened (heavy) cream
1 cup (250ml) milk
½ cup (110g) caster (superfine) sugar
1 vanilla bean, split lengthways
3 egg yolks
2 tablespoons cornflour (cornstarch)
80g (2½ ounces) unsalted butter, chopped

1 Process flour, icing sugar and chopped butter until crumbly. Add egg yolk and enough of the water until ingredients come together. Knead on floured surface until smooth. Enclose in plastic wrap; refrigerate 30 minutes.
2 Grease 10cm x 34cm (4-inch x 13½-inch) loose-based fluted flan tin; place tin on oven tray. Roll pastry between sheets of baking paper until large enough to line tin. Lift pastry into tin; press into base and sides, trim edges. Cover; refrigerate 30 minutes.
3 Preheat oven to 180°C/350°F.
4 Line pastry with baking paper, fill with dried beans or rice. Bake 10 minutes. Remove paper and beans; bake about 10 minutes or until browned. Cool.
5 Meanwhile, make crème pâtissière.
6 Increase oven to 220°C/425°F. Place nectarines in shallow baking dish; sprinkle with juice and brown sugar. Roast 20 minutes or until soft. Cool.
7 Spoon crème pâtissière into pastry case. Cover; refrigerate 30 minutes or until firm. Arrange nectarines on tart; drizzle with pan juices.
crème pâtissière Combine cream, milk and sugar in medium saucepan. Scrape vanilla bean seeds into pan, add pod; bring to the boil. Remove from heat; discard pod. Beat egg yolks in small bowl with electric mixer until thick and creamy; beat in cornflour. Gradually beat in hot cream mixture. Strain into same cleaned saucepan; stir over heat until mixture boils and thickens. Remove from heat; whisk in butter. Cover surface with plastic wrap; cool to room temperature.
prep + cook time 1 hour (+ refrigeration) **serves** 8
nutritional count per serving 40.3g total fat (25.4g saturated fat); 3022kJ (723 cal); 81.7g carbohydrate; 8.6g protein; 5.2g fibre
tip It is fine to use just one 300ml carton of cream for this recipe.

Chocolate soufflé

⅓ cup (75g) caster (superfine) sugar
50g (1½ ounces) butter
1 tablespoon plain (all-purpose) flour
200g (6½ ounces) dark eating (semi-sweet) chocolate, melted
2 eggs, separated
2 egg whites
1 tablespoon cocoa powder

1 Preheat oven to 180°C/350°F. Grease four ¾-cup (180ml) soufflé dishes. Sprinkle inside of dishes with a little of the sugar; shake away excess. Place dishes on oven tray.
2 Melt butter in small saucepan, add flour; cook, stirring, about 2 minutes or until mixture thickens and bubbles. Remove from heat; stir in chocolate and egg yolks. Transfer to large bowl.
3 Beat all egg whites in small bowl with electric mixer until soft peaks form. Gradually add remaining sugar, beating until sugar dissolves. Fold egg white mixture into chocolate mixture, in two batches. Spoon soufflé mixture into dishes.
4 Bake soufflés 15 minutes. Serve immediately, dusted with cocoa powder.

prep + cook time 35 minutes **serves** 4
nutritional count per serving 27.1g total fat (16.1g saturated fat); 2040kJ (488 cal); 52.3g carbohydrate; 8.1g protein; 0.7g fibre
tips Egg whites are vital to a soufflé's success. They must be folded very carefully into the mixture. Use a wide-topped bowl so folding is easier for you. Use a whisk, spatula or large metal spoon for the folding – the choice is yours. Some cooks like to fold a small amount of the egg white (about a quarter) through the flavoured, more solid mixture first to "let the mixture down" a little. Fold in the remaining egg whites, in one or two batches depending on the quantity. Experiment a little to determine what works best for you and your soufflés.
Soufflés must be made just before serving.

Rich chocolate meringue cake

8 egg whites
1 cup (220g) caster (superfine) sugar
60g (2 ounces) dark eating (semi-sweet) chocolate, chopped finely
¼ cup (60g) finely chopped glacé figs
¼ cup (50g) finely chopped seeded prunes
¾ cup (45g) stale breadcrumbs
¼ cup (25g) cocoa powder
1 tablespoon icing (confectioners') sugar
1 tablespoon cocoa powder, extra

1 Preheat oven to 120°C/250°F. Grease 22cm (9-inch) springform tin; line base and side with baking paper.
2 Beat egg whites in medium bowl with electric mixer until soft peaks form. Add sugar, 1 tablespoon at a time, beating until sugar dissolves between additions. Fold in chocolate, fruit, breadcrumbs and sifted cocoa. Spoon mixture into tin.
3 Bake cake about 1½ hours. Cool in oven with door ajar.
4 Dust cake with combined sifted icing sugar and extra cocoa; top with cream, if you like.

prep + cook time 1 hour 45 minutes **serves** 8
nutritional count per serving 3.1g total fat (2.5g saturated fat); 514kJ (123 cal); 44.8g carbohydrate; 5.9g protein; 2.3g fibre
tip This cake is fragile, which is why we've baked it in a springform tin. There's no need to turn it right-side up.

Flourless chocolate hazelnut cake

⅓ cup (35g) cocoa powder
⅓ cup (80ml) hot water
155g (5 ounces) dark eating (semi-sweet) chocolate, melted
155g (5 ounces) butter, melted
1 ⅓ cups (295g) firmly packed light brown sugar
1 cup (100g) ground hazelnuts
4 eggs, separated
1 tablespoon cocoa powder, extra

1 Preheat oven to 180°C/350°F. Grease deep 20cm (8-inch) round cake pan; line base and side with baking paper.
2 Blend cocoa with the water in large bowl until smooth. Stir in chocolate, butter, sugar, ground hazelnuts and egg yolks.
3 Beat egg whites in small bowl with electric mixer until soft peaks form; fold into chocolate mixture in two batches. Pour mixture into pan.
4 Bake cake about 1 hour. Stand cake in pan 15 minutes before turning, top-side up, onto wire rack to cool. Dust with sifted extra cocoa.

prep + cook time 1 hour 20 minutes (+ cooling) **serves** 8
nutritional count per serving 32.8g total fat (17.4g saturated fat); 2132kJ (510 cal); 48.9g carbohydrate; 7.2g protein; 2.4g fibre
tips Ground almonds can be used instead of ground hazelnuts.
This cake rises because of the air beaten into the egg whites. Fold the egg whites into the chocolate mixture very gently to keep the bubbles from collapsing and causing the cake to be flat and heavy.
Store in an airtight container, in the refrigerator, for up to two days.
Suitable to freeze for up to three months.

Apricot and honey soufflés

¼ cup (55g) caster (superfine) sugar
4 fresh medium apricots (200g)
¼ cup (60ml) water
2 tablespoons honey
4 egg whites
1 tablespoon icing (confectioners') sugar

1 Preheat oven to 180°C/350°F. Grease six ¾-cup (180ml) soufflé dishes. Sprinkle inside of dishes with a little of the caster sugar; shake away excess. Place dishes on oven tray.
2 Place apricots in small heatproof bowl, cover with boiling water; stand 2 minutes. Drain; cool 5 minutes. Peel and seed apricots; chop flesh finely.
3 Combine apricot in small saucepan with remaining caster sugar, the water and honey; bring to the boil. Reduce heat; simmer, uncovered, about 10 minutes or until apricots soften to a jam-like consistency.
4 Beat egg whites in small bowl with electric mixer until soft peaks form. With motor operating, gradually add hot apricot mixture, beating until just combined. Spoon mixture into dishes.
5 Bake soufflés about 15 minutes. Serve immediately, dusted with sifted icing sugar.

prep + cook time 35 minutes **serves** 6
nutritional count per serving 0.1g total fat (0g saturated fat); 242kJ (58 cal); 21g carbohydrate; 2.6g protein; 0.6g fibre
tips Egg whites are vital to a soufflé's success. They must be folded very carefully into the mixture. Use a wide-topped bowl so folding is easier for you. Use a whisk, spatula or large metal spoon for the folding – the choice is yours. Some cooks like to fold a small amount of the egg white (about a quarter) through the flavoured, more solid mixture first to "let the mixture down" a little. Fold in the remaining egg whites, in one or two batches depending on the quantity. Experiment a little to determine what works best for you and your soufflés.
Soufflés must be made just before serving.

Chocolate ganache and raspberry cake

⅓ cup (35g) cocoa powder
⅓ cup (80ml) water
150g (4½ ounces) dark eating (semi-sweet) chocolate, melted
150g (4½ ounces) butter, melted
1⅓ cups (300g) firmly packed light brown sugar
1 cup (120g) ground almonds
4 eggs, separated
200g (6½ ounces) dark eating (semi-sweet) chocolate, chopped coarsely
⅔ cup (160ml) thickened (heavy) cream
300g (9½ ounces) raspberries

1 Preheat oven to 160°C/325°F. Grease deep 22cm (9-inch) round cake pan; line base and side with baking paper.
2 Blend sifted cocoa with the water in large bowl until smooth. Stir in melted chocolate, butter, sugar, ground almonds and egg yolks.
3 Beat egg whites in small bowl with electric mixer until soft peaks form. Fold egg whites into chocolate mixture, in two batches. Pour mixture into pan.
4 Bake cake about 1¼ hours. Stand cake in pan 15 minutes; turn, top-side up, onto wire rack to cool.
5 Stir chopped chocolate and cream in small saucepan over low heat until smooth.
6 Place raspberries on top of cake; drizzle chocolate mixture over raspberries. Stand cake at room temperature until chocolate sets.

prep + cook time 1 hour 50 minutes **serves** 12
nutritional count per serving 31.3g total fat (16.1g saturated fat); 2031kJ (486 cal); 45.7g carbohydrate; 7g protein; 2.7g fibre

Soft-centred chocolate cakes

185g (6 ounces) dark eating (semi-sweet) chocolate, chopped coarsely
185g (6 ounces) butter, chopped coarsely
3 egg yolks
⅓ cup (50g) plain (all-purpose) flour
4 eggs
⅓ cup (75g) caster (superfine) sugar
350g (11 ounces) cherry jam

1 Preheat oven to 180°C/350°F. Grease and flour six-hole (¾-cup/180ml) texas muffin pan. Line pan holes with two criss-crossed 5cm x 20cm (2-inch x 8-inch) strips of baking paper.
2 Stir chocolate and butter in small saucepan over low heat until smooth. Transfer mixture to large bowl; stir in egg yolks and sifted flour.
3 Beat eggs and sugar in small bowl with electric mixer until light and fluffy and sugar dissolved. Fold into chocolate mixture. Spoon mixture into pan holes.
4 Bake cakes about 10 minutes; cakes should be soft in the centre. Stand cakes in pan 5 minutes; remove carefully from pan.
5 Meanwhile, melt jam in small saucepan over low heat; blend until smooth, strain. Return jam to saucepan, add a little water to give pouring consistency; bring to the boil. Skim surface; stand 5 minutes.
6 Serve warm cakes drizzled with warm sauce.

prep + cook time 35 minutes **makes** 6
nutritional count per serving 41g total fat (27.2g saturated fat); 2688kJ (643 cal); 74.9g carbohydrate; 8.5g protein; 2.5g fibre
tip To get just the right amount of gooey mixture in the middle of these cakes will take a little experimenting. Every oven has its own personality, and only you can work out the exact timing for these cakes – both in the baking and the standing. Be careful when you're removing the cakes from the pan, the gooey middle is uncooked – but very hot – cake mixture.

Mixed berry cake with vanilla bean syrup

125g (4 ounces) butter, chopped
1 cup (220g) caster (superfine) sugar
3 eggs
½ cup (75g) plain (all-purpose) flour
¼ cup (35g) self-raising flour
½ cup (60g) ground almonds
⅓ cup (80g) sour cream
1 ½ cups (225g) frozen mixed berries
½ cup (100g) drained canned seeded black cherries
vanilla bean syrup
½ cup (110g) caster (superfine) sugar
½ cup (125ml) water
2 vanilla beans

1 Preheat oven to 180°C/350°F. Grease 20cm (8-inch) baba pan well.
2 Beat butter and sugar in small bowl with electric mixer until light and fluffy. Beat in eggs, one at a time. Transfer mixture to large bowl; stir in sifted flours, ground almonds, sour cream, berries and cherries. Pour mixture into pan.
3 Bake cake about 40 minutes.
4 Meanwhile, make vanilla bean syrup.
5 Stand cake in pan 5 minutes; turn onto wire rack set over tray. Pour hot syrup over hot cake.
vanilla bean syrup Place sugar and the water in small saucepan. Split vanilla beans in half lengthways; scrape seeds into pan then add pods. Stir over heat, without boiling, until sugar dissolves. Simmer, uncovered, without stirring, 5 minutes. Using tongs, remove pods from syrup.

prep + cook time 1 hour **serves** 8
nutritional count per serving 23.2g total fat (12g saturated fat); 1233kJ (295 cal); 55.7g carbohydrate; 6.2g protein; 2.9g fibre
tip If you don't have a baba pan, you can use a 20cm (8-inch) round cake pan; grease and line the base and side with baking paper.

Chocolate mocha dacquoise terrine

4 egg whites
1 cup (220g) caster (superfine) sugar
2 tablespoons cocoa powder
200g (6½ ounces) dark eating (semi-sweet) chocolate, chopped coarsely
¾ cup (180ml) pouring cream
2 teaspoons cocoa powder, extra

mocha butter cream
1 tablespoon instant coffee granules
2 tablespoons boiling water
100g (3½ ounces) unsalted butter, softened
2¼ cups (360g) icing (confectioners') sugar

1 Preheat oven to 150°C/300°F. Line three oven trays with baking paper; draw a 10cm x 25cm (4-inch x 10-inch) rectangle on each piece of paper.
2 Beat egg whites in medium bowl with electric mixer until soft peaks form. Gradually add sugar, beating after each addition until sugar dissolves; fold in sifted cocoa. Spread meringue mixture evenly over drawn rectangles.
3 Bake meringues about 45 minutes or until dry. Turn off oven; cool meringues in oven with door ajar.
4 Meanwhile, stir chocolate and cream in small saucepan over low heat until smooth; transfer to small bowl. Refrigerate until firm. Beat chocolate mixture with electric mixer 20 seconds or until changed in colour.
5 Make mocha butter cream.
6 Place one meringue layer on serving plate; spread with half the chocolate mixture, then top with half the butter cream. Top with another meringue layer; spread with remaining chocolate mixture, then remaining butter cream. Top with last meringue layer. Cover; refrigerate 3 hours or overnight. Serve dusted with extra sifted cocoa powder.
mocha butter cream Dissolve coffee in the boiling water in small bowl; cool 10 minutes. Beat butter in small bowl with electric mixer until pale in colour; gradually beat in sifted icing sugar. Beat in coffee mixture.

prep + cook time 1 hour (+ refrigeration & cooling) **serves** 12
nutritional count per serving 18.4g total fat (11.8g saturated fat); 1680kJ (402 cal); 59.7g carbohydrate; 2.7g protein; 0.3g fibre
tip Most ovens only have two oven racks. In fan-forced ovens, it's fine to bake the third meringue on the floor of the oven. After the first 19 minutes of baking, alternate the top meringue to the oven floor position and lower the oven temperature; alternate the top two meringues after 10 minutes. The need to rotate the meringues will depend how evenly your oven bakes.

Pear, chocolate and almond galette

80g (2½ ounces) dark eating (semi-sweet) chocolate, chopped finely
¼ cup (30g) ground almonds
1 sheet puff pastry
1 tablespoon milk
1 medium pear (230g)
1 tablespoon raw sugar

1 Preheat oven to 220°C/425°F. Grease and line oven tray with baking paper.
2 Combine chocolate and 2 tablespoons of the ground almonds in small bowl.
3 Cut pastry sheet into quarters; place quarters on oven tray, prick each with a fork, brush with milk. Divide chocolate mixture over pastry squares, leaving 2cm (¾-inch) border.
4 Peel and core pear; cut into quarters. Cut each pear quarter into thin slices then spread one sliced pear quarter across each pastry square; sprinkle with sugar then remaining ground almonds.
5 Bake galettes about 15 minutes.

prep + cook time 20 minutes **makes** 4
nutritional count per galette 19.9g total fat (11g saturated fat); 1480kJ (354 cal); 38.4g carbohydrate; 5g protein; 3.5g fibre

Chocolate raspberry tart

¾ cup (240g) raspberry jam (conserve)
200g (6½ ounces) dark eating (semi-sweet) chocolate, chopped finely
25g (¾ ounce) unsalted butter, melted
⅔ cup (160ml) pouring cream, warmed
120g (4 ounces) raspberries
sweet pastry
1¼ cups (185g) plain (all-purpose) flour
½ cup (80g) icing (confectioners') sugar
125g cold unsalted butter, chopped coarsely
¼ cup (60ml) iced water, approximately

1 Make sweet pastry.
2 Grease 12.5cm x 35cm (4½-inch x 14-inch) loose-based fluted flan tin. Roll pastry between sheets of baking paper until large enough to line tin. Ease pastry into tin, press into base and side; trim edge, prick base with fork. Cover; refrigerate 30 minutes.
3 Preheat oven to 200°C/400°F.
4 Place tin on oven tray; line pastry with baking paper, fill with dried beans or uncooked rice. Bake 15 minutes. Remove paper and beans; bake about 10 minutes. Spread jam over pastry base; bake further 2 minutes. Cool.
5 Whisk chocolate, butter and cream in medium bowl until smooth. Pour mixture into pastry case; refrigerate 2 hours.
6 Serve tart topped with raspberries.
sweet pastry Process flour, icing sugar and butter until crumbly; add enough of the water to make ingredients come together. Knead dough gently on floured surface until smooth. Enclose in plastic wrap; refrigerate 30 minutes.

prep + cook time 40 minutes (+ refrigeration) **serves** 12
nutritional count per serving 21g total fat (13.4g saturated fat); 1559kJ (373 cal); 42.4g carbohydrate; 3g protein; 1.6g fibre
tip You could also use a 24cm (9½-inch) round loose-based flan tin.

Mini chocolate yule logs (bûches au chocolat)

1 cup (150g) seeded dried dates
1 cup (190g) seeded prunes
1 cup (200g) dried figs
1 cup (140g) brazil nuts
2 eggs
½ cup (110g) firmly packed light brown sugar
1 tablespoon dark rum
100g (3½ ounces) butter, melted
⅓ cup (50g) plain (all-purpose) four
¼ cup (35g) self-raising flour
100g (3½ ounces) dark eating (semi-sweet) chocolate, melted
1 tablespoon icing (confectioners') sugar

chocolate ganache
200g (6½ ounces) dark eating (semi-sweet) chocolate, chopped
½ cup (125ml) pouring cream

1 Preheat oven to 150°C/300°F. Grease eight, cleaned cans (see tip); line with baking paper. Chop fruit and nuts finely; combine in large bowl.
2 Beat eggs and sugar in small bowl with electric mixer until thick and creamy. Add rum, butter and sifted flours; beat until combined. Stir egg mixture into fruit mixture. Push mixture firmly into cans; place on oven tray.
3 Bake cakes about 30 minutes. Turn top-side up onto wire rack to cool.
4 Meanwhile, make chocolate ganache.
5 Line tray with baking paper; spread melted chocolate into 26cm (10½-inch) square. Refrigerate until set.
6 Cut four of the cakes in half crossways. Sandwich one large cake and one half cake, end-to-end, together with ganache. Repeat with remaining large cakes and three of the halves of remaining cake to make four logs.
7 Trim bottom corner from each of the remaining cake halves. Attach to sides of long cakes with ganache.
8 Place logs on boards or plates; spread all over with ganache. Break chocolate into small pieces, gently push into ganache. Refrigerate until set. Serve dusted with sifted icing sugar.
chocolate ganache Stir ingredients in small bowl over small saucepan of simmering water until smooth. Refrigerate 30 minutes, stirring occasionally, until spreadable.

prep + cook time 1 hour 15 minutes (+ cooling & refrigeration) **makes** 4
nutritional count per log 82.9g total fat (41.3g saturated fat); 6278kJ (1502 cal); 166.8g carbohydrate; 18.8g protein; 19.2g fibre
tip We baked these cakes in eight 170g (5½-ounce) passionfruit pulp cans (5.5cm x 8.5cm/2-inch x 3½-inch). Open the cans with an opener that removes the rims (ring-pull cans are not suitable). Freeze pulp for another use. Remove and discard the label from cans; wash and dry cans well.

Passionfruit curd sponge cakes

3 eggs
½ cup (110g) caster (superfine) sugar
¾ cup (110g) self-raising flour
20g (¾ ounce) butter
¼ cup (60ml) boiling water

passionfruit curd

⅓ cup (80ml) passionfruit pulp
½ cup (110g) caster (superfine) sugar
2 eggs, beaten lightly
125g (4 ounces) unsalted butter, chopped coarsely

1 Make passionfruit curd.
2 Preheat oven to 180°C/350°F. Grease 12-hole (½ cup/125ml) oval friand pan with softened butter; dust lightly with flour.
3 Beat eggs in small bowl with electric mixer until thick and creamy. Gradually add sugar, beating until dissolved between additions. Transfer mixture to large bowl. Fold in sifted flour then combined butter and the boiling water. Spoon mixture into pan holes.
4 Bake cakes about 12 minutes. Working quickly, loosen edges of cakes from pan using a small knife; turn immediately onto baking-paper-covered wire racks to cool.
5 Split cooled cakes in half. Spread cut-sides with curd; replace tops. Serve dusted with a little sifted icing sugar.
passionfruit curd Stir ingredients in medium heatproof bowl over pan of simmering water about 10 minutes or until mixture coats the back of a wooden spoon. Cover; refrigerate 3 hours.

prep + cook time 40 minutes (+ refrigeration & cooling) **makes** 12
nutritional count per cake 12.2g total fat (7.2g saturated fat); 957kJ (229 cal); 25.3g carbohydrate; 3.9g protein; 1.2g fibre
tip You will need about four passionfruit for this recipe.

Chocolate mousse cake with coffee anglaise

6 eggs, separated
½ cup (80g) icing (confectioners') sugar
¼ cup (25g) cocoa powder
2 tablespoons cornflour (cornstarch)
150g (4½ ounces) dark eating (semi-sweet) chocolate, melted
1 tablespoon water
1 litre (4 cups) thickened (heavy) cream
600g (1¼ pounds) dark eating (semi-sweet) chocolate, melted, extra

coffee anglaise
3 cups (750ml) milk
1½ cups (135g) coffee beans
8 egg yolks
¾ cup (165g) caster (superfine) sugar

1 Make coffee anglaise.
2 Preheat oven to 180°C/350°F. Grease 25cm x 30cm (10-inch x 12-inch) swiss roll pan; cover base and short sides of pan with baking paper, extending paper 5cm (2 inches) above edges.
3 Beat egg yolks and icing sugar in small bowl with electric mixer until light and creamy. Transfer to large bowl. Fold in sifted cocoa powder and cornflour, then chocolate; stir in the water.
4 Beat egg whites in medium bowl with electric mixer until soft peaks form; fold into chocolate mixture, in two batches. Spread mixture into pan.
5 Bake cake about 15 minutes. Turn cake onto baking-paper-covered wire rack; cool to room temperature.
6 Cut out circle of cake large enough to fit 26cm (10½-inch) springform tin, using smaller pieces to fit, if necessary. Beat cream in large bowl with electric mixer until slightly thickened. Fold in slightly cooled extra melted chocolate in four batches. Pour mixture over cake base, refrigerate until set.
7 Remove cake from tin, dust with a little extra sifted cocoa, if you like; serve with coffee anglaise.
coffee anglaise Bring milk and beans to the boil in large saucepan; cool, covered, 1 hour. Whisk egg yolks and sugar in large bowl, whisk in milk mixture. Return mixture to same pan, stir over heat, without boiling, until slightly thickened, strain; cool to room temperature. Cover; refrigerate until cold.

prep + cook time 1 hour 15 minutes (+ cooling & refrigeration)
serves 10
nutritional count per serving 69.2g total fat (41.4g saturated fat); 4126kJ (987 cal); 80.9g carbohydrate; 15.7g protein; 1.3g fibre

Chocolate marquise

100g (3 ounces) dark eating (semi-sweet) chocolate, chopped coarsely
2 cups (500ml) thickened (heavy) cream
4 egg yolks
2 eggs
½ cup (110g) caster (superfine) sugar
¼ cup (60ml) orange-flavoured liqueur
¾ cup (75g) coarsely grated dark eating (semi-sweet) chocolate
2 teaspoons finely grated orange rind

chocolate sponge
4 eggs
⅔ cup (150g) caster (superfine) sugar
⅓ cup (50g) plain (all-purpose) flour
1 tablespoon cocoa powder

1 Preheat oven to 180°C/350°F; make chocolate sponge.
2 Line base and long sides 14cm x 21cm loaf pan (5½-inch x 8½-inch) with baking paper. Cut two rectangles from cooled sponge: one 13cm x 21cm (5-inch x 8½-inch), and the other 11cm x 19cm (4-inch x 7½-inch). Discard remaining sponge.
3 Stir chopped chocolate and ¾ cup of the cream in small saucepan over low heat until smooth. Beat egg yolks, eggs and sugar in medium bowl with electric mixer until thick and creamy. With motor operating, gradually beat hot chocolate mixture into egg mixture. Cover; refrigerate 30 minutes or until thickened slightly.
4 Meanwhile, beat remaining cream in small bowl with electric mixer until soft peaks form. Fold cream, liqueur, grated chocolate and rind into cooled chocolate mixture.
5 Place smaller sponge rectangle in loaf pan; pour in chocolate mixture, top with remaining sponge rectangle. Cover with foil; freeze until firm.
6 Turn marquise onto board; stand at room temperature about 5 minutes. Slice thickly, serve with fresh berries.
chocolate sponge Grease 25cm x 30cm (10-inch x 12-inch) swiss roll pan; line with baking paper. Beat eggs and sugar in small bowl with electric mixer until thick and creamy; transfer to large bowl. Fold in triple-sifted combined flour and cocoa; spread into pan. Bake 10 minutes. Cool 10 minutes.

prep + cook time 45 minutes (+ refrigeration & freezing) **serves** 10
nutritional count per serving 28.4g total fat (16.4g saturated fat); 1986kJ (475 cal); 44.8g carbohydrate; 7.8g protein; 0.5g fibre

Chocolate mousse

200g (6½ ounces) dark eating (semi-sweet) chocolate, chopped coarsely
30g (1 ounce) unsalted butter
3 eggs, separated
1¼ cups (310ml) thickened (heavy) cream, whipped

1 Melt chocolate and butter in large glass heatproof bowl over large saucepan of simmering water (do not allow water to touch base of bowl). Remove from heat. Stir in egg yolks; cool.
2 Beat egg whites in small bowl with electric mixer until soft peaks form.
3 Meanwhile, fold cream into chocolate mixture; fold in egg whites, in two batches.
4 Spoon mousse mixture into ¾ cup (180ml) serving dishes; refrigerate 3 hours or overnight.

prep + cook time 35 minutes (+ refrigeration) **serves** 6
nutritional count per serving 34.8g total fat (21.4g saturated fat); 1777kJ (425 cal); 22.5g carbohydrate; 6.1g protein; 0.4g fibre
tips The eggs must be at room temperature for success with this recipe. It is fine to use just one 300ml carton of cream for this recipe.
serving suggestion Top with whipped cream and chocolate curls.

Pound cake (quatre quart)

250g (8 ounces) butter, softened
1 cup (220g) caster (superfine) sugar
1 teaspoon vanilla extract
4 eggs
½ cup (75g) self-raising flour
1 cup (150g) plain (all-purpose) flour

1 Preheat oven to 180°C/350°F. Grease deep 20cm (8-inch) round cake pan; line base with baking paper.
2 Beat butter, sugar and extract in small bowl with electric mixer until light and fluffy. Beat in eggs, one at a time. Transfer mixture to large bowl; fold in sifted flours, in two batches. Spread mixture into pan.
3 Bake cake about 1 hour. Stand cake in pan 5 minutes; turn, top-side up, onto wire rack to cool. If you like, dust cake with a little sifted icing (confectioners') sugar.

prep + cook time 1 hour 20 minutes **serves** 12
nutritional count per serving 19.1g total fat (11.8g saturated fat); 1012kJ (242 cal); 31.9g carbohydrate; 4.3g protein; 0.7g fibre
serving suggestion Serve with whipped cream and strawberries.

Poached pears in red wine syrup

6 medium pears (1.4kg)
2 cups (500ml) water
2 cups (500ml) dry red wine
½ cup (125ml) orange-flavoured liqueur
4 strips orange rind
¾ cup (165g) caster (superfine) sugar
1 vanilla bean

1 Peel pears, leaving stems intact.
2 Combine the water, wine, liqueur, rind and sugar in large saucepan. Split vanilla bean in half lengthways; scrape seeds into pan; add pod. Stir over heat, without boiling, until sugar dissolves.
3 Add pears to syrup; bring to the boil. Reduce heat; simmer, covered, about 1 hour or until pears are just tender. Transfer pears to large bowl.
4 Bring syrup to the boil. Reduce heat; simmer, uncovered, about 10 minutes or until syrup reduces by a third. Remove from heat; discard pod. Strain syrup over pears. Cover; refrigerate 2 hours or until cold.
5 Serve pears drizzled with syrup.

prep + cook time 1 hour 20 minutes (+ refrigeration) **serves** 6
nutritional count per serving 0.3g total fat (0g saturated fat); 1028kJ (246 cal); 61g carbohydrate; 0.7g protein; 3.2g fibre
tips We used packham pears for this recipe; they should fit snugly, standing upright, in the saucepan.
If pear syrup is too sweet, you can add about a teaspoon of lemon juice.
You can use Cointreau, Grand Marnier, Curaçao or any other orange-flavoured liqueur in this recipe.

After-dinner treats

Pear and almond friands (financiers)

6 egg whites
185g (6 ounces) butter, melted
1 cup (120g) ground almonds
1 ½ cups (240g) icing (confectioners') sugar
¾ cup (110g) plain (all-purpose) flour
1 small pear (180g), peeled, cored, chopped finely
¼ cup (20g) flaked almonds

1 Preheat oven to 200°C/400°F. Grease 12-hole (⅓-cup/80ml) muffin pan.
2 Whisk egg whites lightly with a fork in medium bowl until frothy. Add butter, ground almonds, sifted icing sugar and flour, then pear; stir until combined.
3 Place ¼-cups of mixture into pan holes; sprinkle with nuts.
4 Bake friands about 20 minutes. Stand in pan 5 minutes; turn, top-side up, onto wire rack to cool.

prep + cook time 35 minutes **makes** 12
nutritional count per friand 19.2g total fat (8.8g saturated fat); 1300kJ (311 cal); 28.8g carbohydrate; 5.3g protein; 1.6g fibre

dOuCEuR

about 1/2c.-

Brandied cherry friands (financiers)

1 cup (150g) frozen seeded cherries
2 tablespoons brandy
1 cup (120g) roasted pecans
6 egg whites
185g (6 ounces) butter, melted
1½ cups (240g) icing (confectioners') sugar
½ cup (75g) plain (all-purpose) flour
cherry sauce
¼ cup (55g) caster (superfine) sugar
2 tablespoons water

1 Preheat oven to 200°C/400°F. Grease 12-hole (½-cup/125ml) oval friand pan.
2 Combine cherries and brandy in small bowl; stand 30 minutes. Drain cherries; reserve liquid.
3 Process nuts until ground finely.
4 Whisk egg whites lightly with fork in medium bowl until combined. Add butter, sifted icing sugar and flour, and nuts; stir until combined. Spoon mixture into pan holes; top with drained cherries.
5 Bake friands about 20 minutes. Stand friands 5 minutes before turning, top-side up, onto serving plates
6 Meanwhile, make cherry sauce.
7 Serve friands with cherry sauce.
cherry sauce Stir sugar, the water and reserved cherry juice in small saucepan over low heat until sugar dissolves. Bring to the boil. Reduce heat; simmer, uncovered, about 3 minutes or until sauce thickens slightly.

prep + cook time 35 minutes (+ standing) **makes** 12
nutritional count per friand 19.9g total fat (8.8g saturated fat); 1363kJ (326 cal); 31g carbohydrate; 3.7g protein; 1.3g fibre

Raspberry and white chocolate friands (financiers)

6 egg whites
185g (6 ounces) butter, melted
1 cup (120g) ground almonds
1 ½ cups (240g) icing (confectioners') sugar
½ cup (75g) plain (all-purpose) flour
100g (3 ounces) white eating chocolate, chopped coarsely
100g (3 ounces) fresh or frozen raspberries

1 Preheat oven to 200°C/400°F. Grease 12-hole (½-cup/125ml) oval friand pan.
2 Whisk egg whites lightly with a fork in medium bowl. Stir in butter, ground almonds and sifted icing sugar and flour. Stir in chocolate. Spoon mixture into pan holes; top each with raspberries.
3 Bake friands about 25 minutes. Stand friands in pans 5 minutes; turn, top-side up, onto wire rack to cool. Dust with a little sifted icing sugar, if you like.

prep + cook time 45 minutes **makes** 12
nutritional count per friand 21g total fat (10.4g saturated fat); 1367kJ (327 cal); 30.1g carbohydrate; 5.3g protein; 1.6g fibre

Crème brûlée praline tarts

1¼ cups (185g) plain (all-purpose) flour
¼ cup (55g) caster (superfine) sugar
125g (4 ounces) cold butter, chopped coarsely
1 egg yolk
1⅓ cups (330ml) pouring cream
⅓ cup (80ml) milk
1 vanilla bean
4 egg yolks
¼ cup (55g) caster (superfine) sugar, extra

praline

¼ cup (55g) caster (superfine) sugar
2 tablespoons water
2 tablespoons roasted unsalted pistachios
1 tablespoon roasted hazelnuts

1 Process flour, sugar and butter until coarse. Add egg yolk; process until combined. Knead on floured surface until smooth. Roll pastry between sheets of baking paper until 4mm (⅛-inch) thick. Refrigerate 15 minutes.
2 Grease six-hole (¾-cup/180ml) texas muffin pan. Cut six 11cm (4-inch) rounds from pastry. Press rounds into pan holes; prick bases with fork. Refrigerate 30 minutes.
3 Preheat oven to 160°C/350°F.
4 Combine cream and milk in small saucepan. Split vanilla bean in half lengthways; scrape seeds into pan (reserve pod for another use). Bring to the boil. Beat egg yolks and extra sugar in small bowl with electric mixer until thick and creamy. Gradually whisk hot cream mixture into egg mixture. Pour warm custard into pastry cases.
5 Bake about 30 minutes or until set; cool 15 minutes. Refrigerate 1 hour.
6 Meanwhile, make praline.
7 Preheat grill (broiler). Remove tarts from pan; place on oven tray. Sprinkle custard with praline; grill until praline caramelises. Serve immediately.
praline Stir sugar and the water in small saucepan over heat until sugar dissolves. Boil, uncovered, without stirring, about 8 minutes or until golden. Place nuts, in single layer, on greased oven tray. Pour toffee over nuts; stand 15 minutes or until set. Break toffee into pieces; process until fine.
prep + cook time 1 hour 15 minutes (+ refrigeration, standing & cooling)
makes 6
nutritional count per tart 49.8g total fat (29.1g saturated fat); 2901kJ (694 cal); 52.8g carbohydrate; 8.7g protein; 1.8g fibre

Madeleines

2 eggs
2 tablespoons caster (superfine) sugar
2 tablespoons icing (confectioners') sugar
¼ cup (35g) self-raising flour
¼ cup (35g) plain (all-purpose) flour
75g (2½ ounces) unsalted butter, melted
1 tablespoon water
2 tablespoons icing (confectioners') sugar, extra

1 Preheat oven to 200°C/400°F. Grease two 12-hole (1½-tablespoon/30ml) madeleine pans.
2 Beat eggs and sifted sugars in small bowl with electric mixer until thick and creamy.
3 Meanwhile, triple-sift flours; sift flour over egg mixture. Pour combined butter and the water down side of bowl then fold ingredients together. Drop rounded tablespoons of mixture into each pan hole.
4 Bake madeleines about 10 minutes. Tap hot pan firmly on bench to release madeleines then turn, top-side down, onto wire rack to cool. Serve dusted with extra sifted icing sugar.

prep + cook time 25 minutes **makes** 24
nutritional count per madeleine 3.1g total fat (1.9g saturated fat); 222kJ (53 cal); 5.4g carbohydrate; 0.9g protein; 0.1g fibre
tip To make orange madeleines, add 1 teaspoon finely grated orange rind when beating the egg mixture. Omit the water and replace with 1 tablespoon orange juice.

Custard and fruit flans

1¾ cups (260g) plain (all-purpose) flour
¼ cup (40g) icing (confectioners') sugar
185g (6 ounces) cold butter, chopped coarsely
1 egg yolk
2 teaspoons iced water, approximately
1 medium kiwifruit (85g)
60g (2 ounces) fresh raspberries, halved
60g (2 ounces) fresh blueberries

custard cream
1 cup (250ml) milk
1 teaspoon vanilla extract
3 egg yolks
⅓ cup (75g) caster (superfine) sugar
2 tablespoons pure cornflour (cornstarch)
⅓ cup (80ml) thickened (heavy) cream, whipped

1 Process flour, sugar and butter until crumbly. With motor operating, add egg yolk and enough of the water to make ingredients come together. Turn dough onto floured surface, knead gently until smooth. Wrap pastry in plastic; refrigerate 30 minutes.
2 Grease two 12-hole (1-tablespoon/20ml) mini muffin pans. Roll out half the pastry between sheets of baking paper until 3mm (⅛-inch) thick. Cut out 12 x 6cm (2¼ inch) rounds; press rounds into holes of one pan. Prick bases of cases well with a fork. Repeat with remaining pastry. Refrigerate 30 minutes.
3 Preheat oven to 200°C/400°F.
4 Bake cases about 12 minutes. Stand cases 5 minutes; transfer to wire rack to cool.
5 Meanwhile, make custard cream.
6 Cut kiwifruit crossways into eight slices; cut 3cm (1¼-inch) rounds from slices. Spoon custard cream into cases; top with fruit.
custard cream Bring milk and extract to the boil in small saucepan. Meanwhile, beat egg yolks, sugar and cornflour in small bowl with electric mixer until thick. With motor operating, gradually beat in hot milk mixture. Return custard to pan; stir over heat until mixture boils and thickens. Cover surface of custard with plastic wrap, refrigerate 1 hour. Fold cream into custard in two batches.

prep + cook time 1 hour (+ refrigeration & cooling) **makes** 24
nutritional count per flan 9.3g total fat (5.6g saturated fat); 627kJ (150 cal); 14.8g carbohydrate; 2.4g protein; 0.7g fibre

Mocha puffs

15g (½ ounce) butter
¼ cup (60ml) water
¼ cup (35g) plain (all-purpose) flour
1 egg

mocha pastry cream
2 teaspoons instant coffee granules
2 teaspoons hot water
1 cup (250ml) milk
60g (2 ounces) dark eating (semi-sweet) chocolate, chopped finely
3 egg yolks
⅓ cup (75g) caster (superfine) sugar
1 tablespoon pure cornflour (cornstarch)

toffee
½ cup (110g) caster (superfine) sugar
¼ cup (60ml) water

1 Preheat oven to 220°C/425°F. Grease two oven trays.
2 Bring butter and the water to the boil in small saucepan. Add flour, beat with wooden spoon over heat until mixture comes away from base and side of the pan and forms a smooth ball.
3 Transfer mixture to small bowl; beat in egg with electric mixer until mixture becomes glossy. Spoon mixture into piping bag fitted with 1cm (½-inch) plain tube. Pipe small rounds, about 5cm (2 inches) apart, on trays; bake 7 minutes. Reduce oven to 180°C/350°F; bake 10 minutes. Cut small hole in side of each puff; bake 5 minutes or until dry to touch. Cool on trays.
4 Meanwhile, make mocha pastry cream and toffee.
5 Spoon pastry cream into piping bag fitted with 5mm (¼-inch) plain tube, pipe through cuts into puffs. Place puffs on foil-lined tray; drizzle with toffee.
mocha pastry cream Dissolve coffee in the water in small jug. Stir milk, chocolate and coffee mixture in small saucepan over heat, until smooth. Bring to the boil. Meanwhile, beat egg yolks, sugar and cornflour in small bowl with electric mixer until thick. With motor operating, gradually beat in hot milk mixture. Return custard to pan; stir over heat until mixture boils and thickens. Cover surface of custard with plastic wrap; refrigerate 1 hour.
toffee Stir ingredients in small pan over heat, without boiling, until sugar dissolves. Bring to the boil; boil, uncovered, without stirring, until golden.
prep + cook time 1 hour (+ refrigeration & cooling) **makes** 24
nutritional count per puff 2.6g total fat (1.3g saturated fat); 171kJ (41 cal); 11.2g carbohydrate; 1.3g protein; 0.1g fibre

Chocolate macaroons (macarons au chocolat)

3 egg whites
¼ cup (55g) caster (superfine) sugar
1 ¼ cups (200g) icing (confectioners') sugar
¾ cup (90g) ground almonds
¼ cup (25g) cocoa powder
dark chocolate ganache
¼ cup (60ml) pouring cream
155g (5 ounces) dark eating (semi-sweet) chocolate, chopped coarsely
1 tablespoon finely crushed buttered brazil nuts

1 Preheat oven to 150°C/300°F. Grease oven trays; line with baking paper.
2 Beat egg whites in small bowl with electric mixer until soft peaks form. Add caster sugar, beat until sugar dissolves; transfer mixture to large bowl. Fold in sifted icing sugar, ground almonds and sifted cocoa, in two batches.
3 Spoon mixture into piping bag fitted with 1cm (½-inch) plain tube. Pipe 4cm (1 ½-inch) rounds about 2.5cm (1 inch) apart onto trays. Tap trays on bench so macaroons spread slightly. Stand 30 minutes.
4 Bake macaroons about 20 minutes. Cool on trays.
5 Meanwhile, make dark chocolate ganache.
6 Sandwich macaroons with ganache.
dark chocolate ganache Bring cream to the boil in small saucepan. Remove from heat; pour over chocolate in small bowl, stir until smooth. Stir in nuts. Stand at room temperature until spreadable.

prep + cook time 45 minutes (+ standing) **makes** 16
nutritional count per macaroon 8.2g total fat (3.2g saturated fat); 665kJ (159 cal); 22.7g carbohydrate; 2.8g protein; 0.7g fibre
tip Buttered brazil nuts are toffee-coated nuts; they're available from nut shops and gourmet food stores.

Coffee hazelnut meringues

2 egg whites
½ cup (110g) caster (superfine) sugar
2 teaspoons instant coffee granules
2 teaspoons hot water
¼ cup (35g) roasted hazelnuts

1 Preheat oven to 120°C/250°F. Grease oven trays; line with baking paper.
2 Beat egg whites in small bowl with electric mixer until soft peaks form. Gradually add sugar, beating until dissolved after each addition.
3 Meanwhile, dissolve coffee in the water in small jug. Fold coffee mixture into egg white mixture.
4 Spoon mixture into piping bag fitted with 5mm (¼-inch) fluted tube. Pipe meringues onto trays about 2cm (¾ inch) apart; top each meringue with a nut.
5 Bake meringues about 45 minutes. Cool meringues in oven with door ajar.

prep + cook time 55 minutes (+ cooling) **makes** 30
nutritional count per meringue 0.7g total fat (0g saturated fat); 100kJ (24 cal); 3.7g carbohydrate; 0.4g protein; 0.1g fibre
tip A piping bag – available from cookware shops – is a really handy thing to have. They are easy to use, much easier than you'd expect, and make the dividing up of a mixture into trays quick and efficient. Buy a few different sizes and shapes of tubes – you'll be surprised how often you'll use them.

White chocolate truffles

1 ½ tablespoons pouring cream
60g (2 ounces) white eating chocolate, chopped coarsely
¼ cup (35g) unsalted pistachios, chopped finely
1 teaspoon coconut-flavoured liqueur
120g (4 ounces) white chocolate melts
1 tablespoon finely chopped unsalted pistachios, extra

1 Stir cream and chocolate in small heatproof bowl over small saucepan of simmering water until smooth (do not let water touch base of bowl). Remove bowl from pan, stir in nuts and liqueur. Cover; refrigerate until firm.
2 Roll level teaspoons of mixture into balls, place on baking-paper-lined tray. Cover; refrigerate until firm.
3 Stir chocolate melts in small heatproof bowl over small saucepan of simmering water until smooth (do not let water touch base of bowl). Remove bowl from pan. Dip chocolate balls into melted chocolate, place on baking-paper-lined tray; sprinkle with extra nuts. Cover; refrigerate until firm.

prep + cook time 20 minutes (+ refrigeration) **serves** 2
nutritional count per serving 47.5g total fat (24.2g saturated fat); 2851kJ (682 cal); 54.2g carbohydrate; 11.1g protein; 2g fibre
tip Truffles can be made two days ahead of time; store in refrigerator.

Coffee walnut creams

1⅔ cups (250g) plain (all-purpose) flour
125g (4 ounces) cold butter, chopped coarsely
¼ cup (55g) caster (superfine) sugar
½ teaspoon vanilla extract
1 egg, beaten lightly
18 walnut halves
walnut butter cream
185g (6 ounces) unsalted butter, softened
¾ cup (120g) icing (confectioners') sugar
1 tablespoon cocoa
1 tablespoon instant coffee granules
1 tablespoon hot water
1¼ cups (125g) walnuts, chopped finely
coffee icing
1 cup (160g) icing (confectioners') sugar
2 teaspoons instant coffee granules
1 tablespoon hot water
1 teaspoon butter

1 Sift flour into medium bowl, rub in butter. Stir in sugar, extract and egg. Knead dough on floured surface until smooth. Divide in half. Roll, each half between sheets of baking paper until 3mm (⅛-inch) thick. Refrigerate 30 minutes.
2 Preheat oven to 180°C/350°F. Grease oven trays; line with baking paper.
3 Using 5.5cm (2-inch) round cutter, cut out 36 rounds from dough. Place on oven trays; bake about 12 minutes. Cool on wire racks.
4 Meanwhile, make walnut butter cream.
5 Sandwich cookies with butter cream; refrigerate 30 minutes.
6 Meanwhile, make coffee icing.
7 Spread cookies with icing and top with walnut halves.
walnut butter cream Beat butter and sifted icing sugar in small bowl with electric mixer until light and fluffy. Beat in combined cocoa, coffee and the water. Stir in nuts.
coffee icing Sift icing sugar into small heatproof bowl, stir in combined coffee and the water; add butter. Stir over small saucepan of simmering water until icing is spreadable.
prep + cook time 1 hour (+ refrigeration) **makes** 18
nutritional count per piece 22g total fat (10g saturated fat); 1308kJ (313 cal); 29.1g carbohydrate; 3.6g protein; 1.3g fibre

Palmiers

2 tablespoons raw sugar
1 sheet puff pastry
1 teaspoon ground nutmeg

1 Preheat oven to 180°C/350°F. Grease two oven trays; line with baking paper.
2 Sprinkle board lightly with a little of the sugar. Roll pastry on sugared board into 20cm x 30cm (8-inch x 12-inch) rectangle; trim edges. Sprinkle pastry with nutmeg and remaining sugar.
3 Starting from long side, loosely roll one side at a time into the middle of the rectangle, so the two long sides meet in the centre. Cut pastry into 1cm (½-inch) thick slices. Place, cut-side up, about 5cm (2 inches) apart, on trays. Spread pastry open slightly at folded ends to make a V-shape.
4 Bake palmiers about 15 minutes or until golden brown; transfer to wire rack to cool.

prep + cook time 35 minutes (+ cooling) **makes** 30
nutritional count per palmier 1.3g total fat (0.1g saturated fat); 105kJ (25 cal); 3.1g carbohydrate; 0.3g protein; 0.1g fibre

Mini white chocolate and raspberry mille-feuilles

1 sheet puff pastry
50g (1 ½ ounces) white eating chocolate, melted
1 tablespoon raspberry jam (conserve)
½ cup (125ml) thickened (heavy) cream
50g (1 ½ ounces) white eating chocolate, grated finely
60g (2 ounces) fresh raspberries
30g (1 ounce) white eating chocolate, chopped coarsely
1 tablespoon thickened (heavy) cream, extra
1 tablespoon icing (confectioners') sugar

1 Preheat oven to 240°C/475°F. Grease oven tray.
2 Place pastry sheet on tray; place a second oven tray on top. Bake about 15 minutes or until pastry is browned and crisp. Cool 2 minutes.
3 Spread pastry with melted chocolate, then jam; cut into 18 rectangles.
4 Beat cream in small bowl with electric mixer until firm peaks form; fold in grated chocolate.
5 Spread cream mixture over jam; sandwich pastry rectangles with raspberries.
6 Stir chopped chocolate and extra cream in small heatproof bowl over small saucepan of simmering water until smooth. Drizzle chocolate mixture over mille-feuilles; dust with sifted icing sugar.

prep + cook time 40 minutes (+ cooling) **makes** 9
nutritional count per mille-feuille 14.3g total fat (6.8g saturated fat); 861kJ (206 cal); 17.4g carbohydrate; 2.3g protein; 0.6g fibre

Apple and prune slice

4 medium apples (600g)
¾ cup (135g) coarsely chopped seeded prunes
2½ cups (625ml) water
½ teaspoon each ground cinnamon and ground nutmeg
2 tablespoons ground hazelnuts
2 sheets shortcrust pastry
1 tablespoon caster (superfine) sugar

1 Peel and core apples; slice thinly. Place apples, prunes and the water in medium saucepan; bring to the boil. Reduce heat; simmer, covered, 10 minutes or until apples are just tender. Drain well; cool 15 minutes.
2 Combine spices and ground hazelnuts in medium bowl; gently stir in apple mixture.
3 Preheat oven to 200°C/400°F. Grease 20cm x 30cm (8-inch x 12-inch) lamington pan; line base with baking paper.
4 Roll one pastry sheet large enough to cover base of pan; place in pan, trim edges. Line pastry with baking paper, fill with dried beans or rice; bake 15 minutes. Remove paper and beans; bake further 5 minutes. Spread apple mixture over pastry.
5 Roll remaining pastry sheet large enough to fit pan; place over apple filling. Brush pastry with a little water, sprinkle with sugar; score pastry in crosshatch pattern.
6 Bake slice about 45 minutes. Cool in pan; cut into squares.

prep + cook time 1 hour 30 minutes (+ cooling) **makes** 24
nutritional count per piece 4.3g total fat (2g saturated fat); 389kJ (93 cal); 12.2g carbohydrate;1.2 g protein; 1.1g fibre

Strawberry meringues

1 egg white
¼ cup (55g) caster (superfine) sugar
2 teaspoons caster (superfine) sugar, extra
1 tablespoon raspberry jam (conserve), warmed, sieved
2 teaspoons orange-flavoured liqueur
75g (2½ ounces) small strawberries, quartered

1 Preheat oven to 120°C/250°F. Place petit four cases on oven tray.
2 Beat egg white and 2 tablespoons of the sugar in small bowl with electric mixer until sugar is dissolved; fold in remaining 1 tablespoon sugar.
3 Drop rounded teaspoons of mixture into cases. Sprinkle meringues with extra sugar.
4 Bake meringues about 25 minutes or until they are dry to touch. Cool meringues in oven with door ajar.
5 Meanwhile, stir jam and liqueur in small saucepan over low heat until warm.
6 Gently press berries into top of each meringue; brush with warm jam mixture. Serve immediately.

prep + cook time 45 minutes **makes** 20
nutritional count per meringue 0g total fat (0g saturated fat); 38kJ (9 cal); 4.4g carbohydrate; 0.2g protein; 0.1g fibre

Vanilla bean thins (langue de chat)

1 vanilla bean
30g (1 ounce) butter, softened
¼ cup (55g) caster (superfine) sugar
1 egg white, beaten lightly
¼ cup (35g) plain (all-purpose) flour

1 Preheat oven to 200°C/400°F. Grease oven trays; line with baking paper.
2 Halve vanilla bean lengthways; scrape seeds into medium bowl, discard pod. Add butter and sugar to bowl; stir until combined. Stir in egg white and sifted flour.
3 Spoon mixture into piping bag fitted with 5mm (¼-inch) plain tube. Pipe 6cm (2¼-inch) long strips (making them slightly wider at both ends) about 5cm (2 inches) apart on trays.
4 Bake biscuits about 5 minutes or until edges are browned lightly; cool on trays.

prep + cook time 25 minutes **makes** 24
nutritional count per biscuit 1g total fat (0.7g saturated fat); 100kJ (24 cal); 3.4g carbohydrate; 0.3g protein; 0.1g fibre

Chocolate hazelnut thins (tuiles au chocolat)

1 egg white
¼ cup (55g) light brown sugar
2 tablespoons plain (all-purpose) flour
2 teaspoons cocoa powder
30g (1 ounce) butter, melted
1 teaspoon milk
1 tablespoon ground hazelnuts

1 Preheat oven to 180°C/350°F. Grease oven trays.
2 Beat egg white in small bowl with electric mixer until soft peaks form; gradually add sugar, beating until sugar dissolves. Stir in sifted flour and cocoa, then butter, milk and ground hazelnuts.
3 Spread level teaspoons of mixture into 8cm (3¼-inch) circles, about 4cm (1½ inches) apart on trays.
4 Bake thins, in batches, about 5 minutes. Remove from tray immediately using metal spatula, place over rolling pin to cool.

prep + cook time 25 minutes **makes** 24
nutritional count per biscuit 1.3g total fat (0.7g saturated fat); 100kJ (24 cal); 3g carbohydrate; 0.4g protein; 0.1g fibre

Kisses.
Music.

Chocolate hazelnut slice

250g (8 ounces) plain chocolate biscuits
60g (2 ounces) butter, melted
4 eggs, separated
¾ cup (165g) caster (superfine) sugar
½ cup (50g) ground hazelnuts
2 tablespoons plain (all-purpose) flour
1 tablespoon cocoa powder

topping

125g (4 ounces) butter, softened
½ cup (110g) caster (superfine) sugar
1 tablespoon orange juice
200g (6½ ounces) dark eating (semi-sweet) chocolate, melted

1 Preheat oven to 180°C/350°F. Grease 20cm x 30cm (8-inch x 12-inch) lamington pan; line with baking paper, extending paper 2cm (¾ inch) over long sides.

2 Process biscuits until fine. Combine 1 cup of the biscuit crumbs with butter in medium bowl; press over base of pan. Refrigerate 10 minutes.

3 Beat egg whites in small bowl with electric mixer until soft peaks form. Gradually add sugar, beating until dissolved between additions; fold in ground hazelnuts, remaining biscuit crumbs and sifted flour. Spread mixture over biscuit base.

4 Bake base about 20 minutes. Cool 20 minutes.

5 Reduce oven to 160°C/325°F.

6 Meanwhile, make topping by beating butter, sugar, egg yolks and juice in small bowl with electric mixer until light and fluffy. Stir in chocolate. Spread mixture over slice.

7 Bake slice about 20 minutes; cool in pan. Refrigerate until firm. Dust with sifted cocoa before cutting.

prep + cook time 1 hour 10 minutes (+ cooling & refrigeration)
makes 24
nutritional count per piece 12.7g total fat (6.8g saturated fat); 732kJ (175 cal); 24.5g carbohydrate; 2.7g protein; 0.6g fibre

Strawberry macaroons (macarons à la fraise)

3 egg whites
¼ cup (55g) caster (superfine) sugar
pink food colouring
2 large (70g) fresh or frozen strawberries
1¼ cups (200g) icing (confectioners') sugar
1 cup (120g) ground almonds
⅓ cup (110g) strawberry jam (conserve)
1 tablespoon icing (confectioners') sugar, extra

1 Preheat oven to 150°C/300°F. Grease oven trays; line with baking paper.
2 Beat egg whites in small bowl with electric mixer until soft peaks form. Add caster sugar and a few drops colouring, beat until sugar dissolves; transfer mixture to large bowl.
3 Meanwhile, push fresh strawberries (or thawed frozen berries) through a fine sieve; you need 1 tablespoon of strawberry puree.
4 Fold sifted icing sugar, ground almonds and strawberry puree into egg white mixture, in two batches.
5 Spoon mixture into piping bag fitted with 1cm (½-inch) plain tube. Pipe 4cm (1½-inch) rounds about 2.5cm (1 inch) apart onto trays. Tap trays on bench so macaroons spread slightly. Stand 30 minutes.
6 Bake macaroons about 20 minutes. Cool on trays.
7 Sandwich macaroons with jam. Dust with extra sifted icing sugar.

prep + cook time 40 minutes (+ standing) **makes** 16
nutritional count per macaroon 4.1g total fat (0.3g saturated fat); 489kJ (117 cal); 21.6g carbohydrate; 2.3g protein; 0.8g fibre

Sauces

French dressing

⅓ cup (80ml) white wine vinegar
2 teaspoons dijon mustard
⅔ cup (160ml) olive oil

1 Whisk vinegar and mustard in small jug until smooth.
2 Gradually whisk in oil, in a thin steady stream, until thickened.

prep time 5 minutes **makes** 1 cup
nutritional count per tablespoon 12.1g total fat (1.7g saturated fat); 456kJ (109 cal); 0g carbohydrate; 0g protein; 0g fibre
tip Add a finely chopped shallot or some fines herbes (see page 11) to give this dressing that little "extra".
serving suggestion This dressing goes well with any type of salad or salad greens.

Classic mayonnaise

2 egg yolks
½ teaspoon salt
1 teaspoon dijon mustard
⅔ cup (160ml) extra light olive oil
⅓ cup (80ml) olive oil
1 tablespoon white wine vinegar
1 tablespoon lemon juice

1 Combine egg yolks, salt and mustard in medium bowl. Gradually add oils in a thin, steady stream, whisking constantly until mixture thickens. Stir in vinegar and juice.

prep time 15 minutes **makes** 1 cup
nutritional count per tablespoon 19.2g total fat (2.9g saturated fat); 719kJ (172 cal); 0g carbohydrate; 0.5g protein; 0g fibre
tips Nothing beats homemade mayonnaise. And if you don't wish to whisk, use a small processor. From this base, you can make endless variations: try adding fresh herbs, rocket, anchovies, crushed garlic or preserved lemon rind.
serving suggestion This sauce goes well with meats and vegetables, as a sandwich filling, salad dressing or dipping sauce.

Aïoli

2 egg yolks
1 teaspoon dijon mustard
1 teaspoon salt
⅔ cup (160ml) extra light olive oil
⅓ cup (80ml) olive oil
4 cloves garlic, quartered
1 tablespoon white wine vinegar
1 tablespoon lemon juice

1 Combine egg yolks, mustard and salt in medium bowl. Gradually add oils in a thin, steady stream, whisking constantly until mixture thickens.
2 Using mortar and pestle, crush garlic and remaining salt to smooth paste. Stir paste, vinegar and juice into mayonnaise.

prep time 20 minutes **makes** 1 cup
nutritional count per tablespoon 19.9g total fat (3g saturated fat); 752kJ (180 cal); 0.2g carbohydrate; 0.6g protein; 0.2g fibre
tips Aïoli comes from the south of France.
Store aïoli in a screw-top jar in the refrigerator for up to three days.
serving suggestion This sauce goes well with grilled fish fillets, crudités, fried or boiled potatoes.

Béchamel sauce

30g (1 ounce) butter
2 tablespoons plain (all-purpose) flour
1¼ cups (310ml) hot milk
pinch nutmeg

1 Melt butter in medium saucepan, add flour; cook, stirring, until mixture bubbles and thickens.
2 Gradually add milk, stirring, until mixture boils and thickens. Stir in nutmeg.

prep + cook time 20 minutes **makes** 1 cup
nutritional count per tablespoon 3.1g total fat (2.1g saturated fat); 176kJ (42 cal); 2.6g carbohydrate; 1.1g protein; 0.1g fibre
serving suggestion Use béchamel in pasta dishes like lasagne, or serve with grilled fish fillets or corned beef.

Béarnaise

2 tablespoons white vinegar
2 tablespoons water
1 shallot (25g), chopped finely
2 teaspoons coarsely chopped fresh tarragon
½ teaspoon black peppercorns
3 egg yolks
200g (6½ ounces) unsalted butter, melted
1 tablespoon finely chopped fresh tarragon

1 Bring vinegar, the water, shallot, coarsely chopped tarragon and peppercorns to the boil in small saucepan. Reduce heat; simmer, uncovered, about 2 minutes or until liquid reduces by half. Strain over medium heatproof bowl; discard solids. Cool 10 minutes.
2 Whisk egg yolks into vinegar mixture until combined. Set bowl over medium saucepan of simmering water; do not let water touch base of bowl. Whisk mixture over heat until thickened.
3 Remove bowl from heat; gradually whisk in melted butter in a thin, steady stream until sauce thickens slightly. Stir in finely chopped tarragon.

prep + cook time 25 minutes **makes** 1 cup
nutritional count per tablespoon 15.1g total fat (9.5g saturated fat); 577kJ (138 cal); 0.2g carbohydrate; 0.8g protein; 0g fibre
serving suggestion This sauce goes well with grilled meat, chicken or fish fillets.

Chicken and mushroom velouté

2¼ cups (560ml) chicken stock
60g (2 ounces) butter
2 tablespoons plain (all-purpose) flour
1 small brown onion (80g), chopped finely
150g (4½ ounces) button mushrooms, sliced thinly
¼ cup (60ml) dry white wine
¼ cup (60ml) pouring cream

1 Place stock in small saucepan; bring to the boil then remove from heat.
2 Melt 40g (1½ ounces) of the butter in medium saucepan, add flour; cook, stirring, about 2 minutes or until mixture bubbles and thickens. Gradually stir in hot stock; bring to the boil. Cook, stirring, until sauce boils and thickens. Reduce heat; simmer, uncovered, about 20 minutes or until reduced by half. Strain sauce into small bowl.
3 Melt remaining butter in medium saucepan; cook onion, stirring, until softened. Add mushrooms; cook, stirring, about 5 minutes or until softened.
4 Add wine to pan; cook, stirring, until almost all liquid evaporates. Add velouté; bring to the boil. Add cream; reduce heat, stir until sauce is heated through.

prep + cook time 35 minutes **makes** 2½ cups
nutritional count per tablespoon 2.6g total fat (1.7g saturated fat); 130kJ (31 cal); 0.9g carbohydrate; 0.6g protein; 0.2g fibre
tips Velouté, which translates from the French as "the texture of velvet", is similar to a béchamel except for the fact that a light stock is added to the roux instead of milk. If you serve this sauce with fish, replace the chicken stock with fish stock; for a vegetarian version, use vegetable stock. Velouté should be served as soon as it is made.
serving suggestion This sauce goes well with pasta and as a chicken and bacon pie filling.

Beurre blanc

¼ cup (60ml) dry white wine
1 tablespoon lemon juice
¼ cup (60ml) pouring cream
125g (4 ounces) cold butter, chopped coarsely

1 Bring wine and juice to the boil in small saucepan. Boil, without stirring, until reduced by two-thirds.
2 Add cream; return to the boil then reduce heat. Whisk in cold butter, piece by piece, whisking between additions, until sauce is smooth and thickened slightly.

prep + cook time 20 minutes **makes** 1 cup
nutritional count per tablespoon 10.4g total fat (6.8g saturated fat); 406kJ (97 cal); 0.3g carbohydrate; 0.2g protein; 0g fibre
serving suggestion This sauce goes well with steamed or grilled salmon and steamed vegetables.

Bordelaise

2 shallots (50g), chopped coarsely
½ teaspoon dried green peppercorns, crushed
2 cups (500ml) dry red wine
1½ cups (375ml) beef stock
1 sprig fresh thyme
2 dried bay leaves
2 stalks fresh flat-leaf parsley
60g (2 ounces) cold unsalted butter, chopped coarsely

1 Combine shallot, pepper and wine in medium saucepan; bring to the boil then reduce heat. Simmer, uncovered, about 15 minutes or until reduced by a third.
2 Add stock, thyme, bay leaves and parsley; bring to the boil then reduce heat. Simmer, uncovered, about 1 hour or until sauce is reduced to ½ cup. Strain, discard herbs.
3 Return sauce to same cleaned pan; stir in butter, piece by piece, over low heat, until sauce is smooth.

prep + cook time 1 hour 35 minutes **makes** ½ cup
nutritional count per tablespoon 8.3g total fat (5.5g saturated fat); 568kJ (136 cal); 0.7g carbohydrate; 1.1g protein; 0.1g fibre
tip This sauce has its origins in the region of Bordeaux so use a merlot here which is comparable to the wines from this region.
serving suggestion This sauce goes well with roast lamb backstraps and fried pork fillets.

Crème anglaise

1 vanilla bean
1 ½ cups (375ml) milk
⅓ cup (75g) caster (superfine) sugar
4 egg yolks

1 Split vanilla bean in half lengthways; scrape seeds into medium saucepan, add pod, milk and one tablespoon of the sugar. Bring to the boil then strain into large jug. Discard pod.
2 Meanwhile, whisk egg yolks and remaining sugar in medium heatproof bowl set over medium saucepan of simmering water (do not allow water to touch base of bowl) until thick and creamy. Gradually whisk in hot milk mixture.
3 Return custard mixture to pan; stir, over low heat, until mixture is just thick enough to coat the back of a spoon.
4 Return custard to bowl; refrigerate about 1 hour or until cold.

prep + cook time 30 minutes (+ refrigeration) **makes** 1 ½ cups
nutritional count per tablespoon 2 .1g total fat (0.9g saturated fat); 184kJ (44 cal); 5.2g carbohydrate; 1.4g protein; 0g fibre
tips Low heat and constant whisking are the key elements to a successful crème anglaise. Try flavouring the custard with liqueurs, finely grated citrus rind, chocolate, spices or coffee.
serving suggestion This sauce goes well with fresh figs, chocolate cake and apple pie.

glossary

almonds

blanched brown skins removed.

flaked paper-thin slices.

ground also called almond meal.

slivered small pieces cut lengthways.

anchovy fillets small oily fish commonly preserved then packed in oil or salt in cans; strong in flavour.

artichokes

globe large flower-bud of a member of the thistle family; it has tough petal-like leaves, and is edible in part when cooked.

hearts tender centre of the globe artichoke; is obtained after the choke is removed. Cooked hearts are available in brine or marinated in oil.

bacon slices also called bacon rashers.

baguette see page 9

baking paper also called parchment paper or baking parchment; a silicone-coated paper used to line baking pans and oven trays.

bay leaves aromatic leaves from the bay tree available fresh or dried; adds a strong, slightly peppery flavour.

beans

broad (fava) also called windsor and horse beans; available dried, fresh, canned and frozen. Fresh should be peeled twice (discard outer green pod and beige-green inner shell); the frozen beans have had their pods removed but the beige shell still needs removal.

butter cans labelled butter beans are, in fact, cannellini beans. Confusingly butter is also another name for lima beans (dried and canned); a large beige bean having a mealy texture and mild taste.

cannellini small white bean similar to other *phaseolus vulgaris* varieties (great northern, navy or haricot). Available dried or canned.

green also called french or string beans; long thin fresh bean is consumed in its entirety once cooked.

white a generic term we use for canned or dried cannellini, haricot, navy or great northern beans.

beef

eye-fillet tenderloin, fillet; fine texture, most expensive, very tender.

scotch fillet cut from the muscle running behind the shoulder along the spine. Also called cube roll, cuts include standing rib roast and rib-eye.

skirt steak lean, flavourful coarse-grained cut from the inner thigh. Needs slow-cooking; good for stews.

beetroot (beets) firm, round root vegetable.

bicarbonate of soda also called baking soda.

breadcrumbs

fresh bread, usually white, processed into crumbs.

packaged prepared fine-textured but crunchy white breadcrumbs; good for coating foods that are to be fried.

brioche French in origin; a rich, yeast-leavened, cake-like bread made with butter and eggs. Available from cake or specialty bread shops.

butter we use salted butter unless stated.

caperberries olive-sized fruit formed after the buds of the caper bush have flowered; they are usually sold pickled in a vinegar brine with stalks intact.

capers grey-green buds of a warm climate shrub, sold dried and salted or pickled in a vinegar brine.

capsicum (bell pepper) also known as pepper. Discard seeds and membranes before use.

cardamom a spice native to India and used extensively in its cuisine; can be purchased in pod, seed or ground form. Has a distinctive aromatic, sweetly rich flavour and is one of the world's most expensive spices.

cayenne pepper a thin-fleshed, long, very hot dried red chilli, usually available ground.

celeriac tuberous root with knobbly brown skin, white flesh and a celery-like flavour. Keep peeled celeriac in acidulated water to stop discolouring. It can be grated and eaten raw in salads; used in soups and stews; boiled and mashed like potatoes; or sliced thinly and deep-fried as chips.

cheese

blue mould-treated cheeses mottled with blue veining. Varieties include firm and crumbly stilton types and mild, creamy brie-like cheeses.

bocconcini from the diminutive of "boccone", meaning mouthful in Italian; walnut-sized, baby mozzarella, a delicate, semi-soft, white cheese. Sold fresh, it spoils rapidly; refrigerate in brine for 1 or 2 days.

brie see page 9

camembert see page 9

cream cheese commonly called philadelphia or philly; a soft cow's-milk cheese, its fat content ranges from 14 to 33 per cent.

goat's made from goat's milk; has an earthy, strong taste. Available soft, crumbly and firm, in various shapes and sizes, and sometimes rolled in ash or herbs.

gruyère a hard-rind Swiss cheese with small holes and a nutty, slightly salty flavour. A popular cheese for soufflés.

parmesan also called parmigiano; a hard, grainy cow's-milk cheese originating in the Parma region of Italy. The curd is salted in brine for a month then aged for up to 2 years.

pizza cheese a commercial blend of varying proportions of processed grated mozzarella, cheddar and parmesan.

roquefort considered the "king of cheeses", this is a blue cheese with a singularly pungent taste; made only from the milk of specially bred sheep and ripened in the damp limestone caves found under the village of Roquefort-sur-Soulzon in France. Has a sticky, bone-coloured rind and, when ripe, the sharp, almost metallic-tasting interior is creamy and almost shiny.

chervil also called cicily; mildly fennel-flavoured member of the parsley family with curly dark-green leaves. Available both fresh and dried but, like all herbs, is best used fresh; it loses its delicate flavour the longer it's cooked.

chicken

breast fillet breast halved, skinned, boned.

drumettes small fleshy part of the wing between shoulder and elbow, trimmed to resemble a drumstick.

tenderloins thin strip of meat lying just under the breast.

thigh cutlets thigh with skin and centre bone intact; sometimes found skinned with bone intact.

thigh fillets thigh with skin and centre bone removed.

chocolate

dark eating (semi-sweet) contains a high percentage of cocoa liquor and cocoa butter, and little added sugar. It is ideal for use in desserts and cakes.

melts small discs of compounded milk, white or dark chocolate ideal for melting and moulding.

white eating contains no cocoa solids but derives its sweet flavour from cocoa butter. Very sensitive to heat.

chorizo small, coarse-textured pork and beef Spanish sausages. They are deeply smoked, highly-spiced and dry-cured so that they do not need cooking.

cinnamon available in pieces (sticks or quills) and ground into powder.

cloves dried flower buds of a tropical tree; used whole or ground. They have a strong scent and taste so use sparingly.

cocoa powder also known as unsweetened cocoa.

cornflour also called cornstarch. Made from corn or wheat.

cornichons see page 8

cranberries available dried and frozen; have a rich, astringent flavour and can be used in cooking sweet and savoury dishes. The dried version can usually be substituted for or with other dried fruit.

cream

pouring also known as pure cream. It has no additives, and contains a minimum fat content of 35 per cent.

thickened (heavy) a whipping cream that contains a thickener (minimum fat content of 35 per cent).

crème fraîche see page 8

cumin also called zeera or comino; resembling caraway in size, cumin is the dried seed of a parsley-related plant with a spicy, almost curry-like flavour. Available dried as seeds or ground.

dill also called dill weed; used fresh or dried, in seed form or ground. Its feathery, frond-like fresh leaves are grassier and more subtle than the dried version or the seeds.

eggplant also called aubergine. Ranging in size from tiny to very large and in colour from pale green to deep purple. Can also be purchased char-grilled, packed in oil, in jars.

eggs we use large (60g) chicken eggs. If a recipe calls for raw or barely cooked eggs, exercise caution if there is a salmonella problem in your area, particularly in food eaten by children and pregnant women.

endive, curly also called frisee, a curly-leafed green vegetable, mainly used in salads.

fennel also called finocchio or anise; a crunchy green vegetable slightly resembling celery. Dried fennel seeds are also available; they have a stronger licorice flavour.

figs are best eaten in peak season, at the height of summer. Vary in skin and flesh colour according to type not ripeness. When ripe, figs should be unblemished and bursting with flesh.

flour

plain unbleached wheat flour is the best for baking: the gluten content ensures a strong dough, which produces a light result.

self-raising plain or wholemeal flour with baking powder and salt added; make at home in the proportion of 1 cup flour to 2 teaspoons baking powder.

gelatine we use dried (powdered) gelatine; it's also available in sheet form called leaf gelatine. Three teaspoons of dried gelatine (8g or one sachet) is about the same as four sheets.

ghee clarified butter; with the milk solids removed, this fat has a high smoking point so can be heated to a high temperature without burning. Used as a cooking medium in Indian recipes.

glacé fruit fruit such as peaches, pineapple, fig and orange cooked in heavy sugar syrup then dried.

honey honey sold in a squeezable container is not suitable for the recipes in this book.

horseradish member of the mustard family, this white root vegetable in pungent in flavour. Commonly purchased at the supermarket in two forms: prepared horseradish (preserved grated root) and horseradish cream (commercially prepared paste consisting of grated horseradish, vinegar, oil and sugar). These cannot be substituted for each other in cooking.

juniper berries dried berries of an evergreen tree; the main flavouring ingredient in gin.

kumara the Polynesian name of an orange-fleshed sweet potato often confused with yam; good baked, boiled, mashed or fried similarly to other potatoes.

lamb

backstrap also known as eye of loin; the larger fillet from a row of loin chops or cutlets. Tender, best cooked rapidly: barbecued or pan-fried.

cutlet small, tender rib chop; sometimes sold french-trimmed, with all the fat and gristle at the narrow end of the bone removed.

leg cut from the hindquarter; can be boned, butterflied, rolled and tied, or cut into dice.

lamb's lettuce also called lamb's lettuce, mache or corn salad; has small, tender velvety leaves. It is sold in punnets and is available from autumn into spring.

lentils du puy see page 8

mayonnaise we use whole-egg mayonnaise; a commercial product of high quality made with whole eggs and labelled as such.

mesclun pronounced mess-kluhn; also called mixed greens or spring salad mix. A commercial blend of assorted young lettuce and other green leaves, including baby spinach leaves, mizuna and curly endive.

milk we use full-cream homogenised milk unless stated otherwise.

mushrooms

button small, cultivated white mushrooms with a mild flavour. When a recipe in this book calls for an unspecified mushroom, use button.

oyster also known as abalone; grey-white mushrooms shaped like a fan. Prized for their smooth texture and subtle, oyster-like flavour.

swiss brown also known as roman or cremini; light to dark brown in colour with a full-bodied flavour.

mustard

dijon see page 8

wholegrain also called seeded. A French-style coarse-grain mustard made from crushed mustard seeds and dijon-style french mustard.

nutmeg a strong and pungent spice ground from the dried nut of a native Indonesian tree. Usually found ground, the flavour is more intense from a whole nut, available from spice shops, so it's best to grate your own. Found in mixed spice mixtures.

oil

cooking spray we use a cholesterol-free spray made from canola oil.

olive made from ripened olives. Extra virgin and virgin are the first and second press, respectively, and are considered the best; the "extra light" or "light" on other types refers to taste not fat levels.

peanut pressed from ground peanuts; the most commonly used oil in Asian cooking because of its high smoke point (capacity to handle high heat without burning).

vegetable any number of oils from plant rather than animal fats.

onion

green also called scallion or (incorrectly) shallot. An immature onion picked before the bulb has formed, it has a long, bright-green edible stalk.

red also called spanish, red spanish or bermuda onion; a sweet-flavoured, large, purple-red onion.

spring crisp, narrow green-leafed tops and a round sweet white bulb larger than green onions.

oregano also called wild marjoram; has a woody stalk and clumps of tiny, dark-green leaves. Has a pungent, peppery flavour.

pine nuts also known as pignoli; not a nut but a small, cream-coloured kernel from pine cones. They are best roasted before use to bring out the flavour.

pistachios green, delicately flavoured nuts inside hard off-white shells. Available salted or unsalted in their shells; you can also get them shelled.

polenta also known as cornmeal; a flour-like cereal made of dried corn (maize). Also the dish made from it.

potato

baby new also called chats; not a separate variety but an early harvest with very thin skin. Good unpeeled steamed, eaten hot or cold in salads.

bintje oval, creamy skin, yellow flesh; good all-purpose potato, great baked and fried, good in salads.

desiree oval, pink-skinned, waxy yellow flesh; good in salads, boiled and roasted.

kipfler (fingerling) small, finger-shaped, nutty flavour; great baked and in salads.

lasoda round, red skin with deep eyes, white flesh; good for mashing or roasting.

pink-eye small, off-white skin, deep purple eyes; good steamed and boiled, great baked.

russet burbank long and oval, rough white skin with shallow eyes, white flesh; good for baking and frying.

sebago white skin, oval; good fried, mashed and baked.

quail related to the pheasant and partridge; a small, delicate-flavoured farmed game bird ranging in weight from 250g to 300g.

rhubarb a plant with long, green-red stalks; becomes sweet and edible when cooked.

roasting/toasting nuts and dried coconut can be roasted in the oven to restore their fresh flavour and release aromatic oils; spread evenly onto an oven tray, roast in a moderate oven about 5 minutes. Desiccated coconut, pine nuts and sesame seeds roast more evenly if stirred over low heat in a heavy-based frying pan; their natural oils help turn them golden.

rocket (arugula) also called rucola; peppery green leaf eaten raw or used in cooking. Baby rocket leaves are smaller and less peppery.

saffron stigma of a member of the crocus family, available ground or in strands; imparts a yellow-orange colour to food once infused. The quality can vary greatly; the best is the most expensive spice in the world.

seafood

mussels should only be bought from a reliable fish market: they must be tightly closed when bought, indicating they are alive. Before cooking, scrub shells with a strong brush to remove beards; do not eat any that do not open after cooking.

prawns (shrimp) can be bought uncooked (green) or cooked, with or without shells.

scallops a type of bivalve; often eaten raw or barely seared, they should never be cooked more than 30 seconds as they will lose their juicy tenderness and be tough.

white fish non-oily fish; includes bream, flathead, whiting, snapper, redfish, dhufish and ling.

shallots see page 9

silver beet (swiss chard) also known, incorrectly, as spinach; has fleshy stalks and large leaves.

spinach also called english spinach and incorrectly, silver beet. Baby spinach leaves are best eaten raw in salads; the larger leaves should be added last to soups, stews and stir-fries, and should be cooked until barely wilted.

sugar

brown a soft, finely granulated sugar retaining molasses for colour and flavour.

caster also called superfine or finely granulated table sugar.

icing (confectioners') also called powdered sugar; pulverised granulated sugar crushed together with a small amount of cornflour.

pure icing (confectioners') also called powdered sugar.

raw natural brown granulated sugar.

tarragon french tarragon has a subtle aniseed flavour; it is one of the herbs that make up fines herbes.

tomato

canned whole peeled tomatoes in natural juices; available crushed, chopped or diced. Use undrained.

cherry also called tiny tim or tom thumb; small and round.

egg (plum) also called roma; smallish, oval-shaped tomatoes.

paste triple-concentrated tomato puree used to flavour soups, stews, sauces and casseroles.

puree canned pureed tomatoes (not tomato paste); substitute with fresh peeled and pureed tomatoes.

semi-dried partially dried tomato pieces in olive oil; softer and juicier than sun-dried, these are not preserved so do not keep as long as sun-dried.

sun-dried tomato pieces dried with salt; this dehydrates the tomato, concentrating the flavour. We use sun-dried tomatoes in oil, unless stated otherwise.

turmeric also called kamin; is a rhizome related to galangal and ginger. Must be grated or pounded to release its acrid aroma and pungent flavour. Known for the golden colour it imparts, fresh turmeric can be substituted with the more commonly found dried powder.

vanilla

bean dried, long, thin pod; the minuscule black seeds inside are used to impart a vanilla flavour.

extract obtained from vanilla beans infused in water; a non-alcoholic version of essence.

vinegar

balsamic originally from Modena, Italy, there are now many on the market ranging in pungency and quality. Quality can be determined up to a point by price; use the most expensive sparingly.

cider made from fermented apples.

sherry a natural vinegar made from the sherry grape grown in the southwest of Spain; aged in oak, this traditional wine vinegar has a mellow sweet-sour taste, similar to balsamic vinegar.

wine made from red or white wine.

watercress one of the cress family, a large group of peppery greens used raw in salads, dips and sandwiches, or cooked in soups. Highly perishable, so it must be used as soon as possible after purchase.

witlof (belgian endive) related to and confused with chicory. A versatile vegetable, it tastes good cooked and raw.

worcestershire sauce thin, dark-brown spicy sauce; used as a seasoning for meat, gravies and cocktails, and as a condiment.

zucchini also called courgette; harvested when young, its edible flowers can be stuffed and deep-fried.

index

conversion chart

MEASURES

One Australian metric measuring cup holds approximately 250ml, one Australian metric tablespoon holds 20ml, one Australian metric teaspoon holds 5ml.

The difference between one country's measuring cups and another's is within a two- or three-teaspoon variance, and will not affect your cooking results. North America, New Zealand and the United Kingdom use a 15ml tablespoon.

All cup and spoon measurements are level. The most accurate way of measuring dry ingredients is to weigh them. When measuring liquids, use a clear glass or plastic jug with the metric markings.

We use large eggs with an average weight of 60g.

LIQUID MEASURES

METRIC	IMPERIAL
30ml	1 fluid oz
60ml	2 fluid oz
100ml	3 fluid oz
125ml	4 fluid oz
150ml	5 fluid oz (¼ pint/1 gill)
190ml	6 fluid oz
250ml	8 fluid oz
300ml	10 fluid oz (½ pint)
500ml	16 fluid oz
600ml	20 fluid oz (1 pint)
1000ml (1 litre)	1¾ pints

LENGTH MEASURES

METRIC	IMPERIAL
3mm	⅛in
6mm	¼in
1cm	½in
2cm	¾in
2.5cm	1in
5cm	2in
6cm	2½in
8cm	3in
10cm	4in
13cm	5in
15cm	6in
18cm	7in
20cm	8in
23cm	9in
25cm	10in
28cm	11in
30cm	12in (1ft)

DRY MEASURES

METRIC	IMPERIAL
15g	½oz
30g	1oz
60g	2oz
90g	3oz
125g	4oz (¼lb)
155g	5oz
185g	6oz
220g	7oz
250g	8oz (½lb)
280g	9oz
315g	10oz
345g	11oz
375g	12oz (¾lb)
410g	13oz
440g	14oz
470g	15oz
500g	16oz (1lb)
750g	24oz (1½lb)
1kg	32oz (2lb)

OVEN TEMPERATURES

The oven temperatures in this book are for conventional ovens;
if you have a fan-forced oven, decrease the temperature by 10-20 degrees.

	°C (CELSIUS)	°F (FAHRENHEIT)
Very slow	120	250
Slow	150	300
Moderately slow	160	325
Moderate	180	350
Moderately hot	200	400
Hot	220	425
Very hot	240	475

First published in 2011 by ACP Magazines Ltd,
a division of Nine Entertainment Co.
54 Park St, Sydney
GPO Box 4088, Sydney, NSW 2001.
phone (02) 9282 8618; fax (02) 9267 9438
acpbooks@acpmagazines.com.au; www.acpbooks.com.au

ACP BOOKS
General Manager - Christine Whiston
Associate Publisher - Seymour Cohen
Editor-in-Chief - Susan Tomnay
Creative Director - Hieu Chi Nguyen
Food Director - Pamela Clark

Published and Distributed in the United Kingdom by Octopus Publishing Group
Endeavour House
189 Shaftesbury Avenue
London WC2H 8JY
United Kingdom
phone (+44)(0)207 632 5400; fax (+44)(0)207 632 5405
info@octopus-publishing.co.uk;
www.octopusbooks.co.uk

Printed by Toppan Printing Co., China

International foreign language rights, Brian Cearnes, ACP Books bcearnes@acpmagazines.com.au

A catalogue record for this book is available from the British Library.
ISBN 978-1-74245-108-4